IMAGES OF ASIA

The Chinese House:
Craft, Symbol, and the Folk Tradition

Series Editors, China Titles:
NIGEL CAMERON, SYLVIA FRASER-LU

The Chinese House
Craft, Symbol, and the Folk Tradition

RONALD G. KNAPP

HONG KONG
OXFORD UNIVERSITY PRESS
OXFORD NEW YORK

Oxford University Press

Oxford New York
Athens   Auckland   Bangkok   Bogota   Bombay
Buenos Aires   Calcutta   Cape Town   Dar es Salaam
Delhi   Florence   Hong Kong   Istanbul   Karachi
Kuala Lumpur   Madras   Madrid   Melbourne
Mexico City   Nairobi   Paris   Singapore
Taipei   Tokyo   Toronto

and associated companies in
Berlin   Ibadan

Oxford is a trademark of Oxford University Press

First published 1990
This impression (lowest digit)
3 5 7 9 10 8 6 4

British Library Cataloguing in Publication Data

Knapp, Ronald G.
The Chinese house: craft, symbol and the folk tradition—
(Images of Asia)
1. China Residences. Architectural features
I. Title   II. Series
728.0951

Library of Congress Cataloging-in-Publication Data

Knapp, Ronald G., 1940–
The Chinese house: craft, symbol, and the folk tradition/
Ronald G. Knapp.
p. cm.—(Images of Asia)
Includes bibliographical references and index.
ISBN 0-19-585115-3
1. Dwellings—China. 2. Dwellings—Taiwan. 3. Vernacular
architecture—China. 4. Vernacular architecture—Taiwan.
5. China—Social life and customs. 6. Taiwan—Social life and customs.
I. Title   II. Series. GT 365.K63 1990
392.36′00951—dc20   90-7665 CIP

Printed in Hong Kong
Published by Oxford University Press (China) Ltd
18/F Warwick House. Taikoo Place, 979 King's Road, Quarry Bay, Hong Kong

Contents

Acknowledgements

THE author gratefully acknowledges with thanks Huang Hanmin, Olivier Laude, Shen Dongqi, the late Paul Sun, and Arthur J. Van Alstyne who have permitted the use of their photographs in this volume. Eleven other illustrations are from Chinese-language sources, and the remaining illustrations are by the author.

The sources of the illustrations are as follows. Plate 1, photo courtesy of Arthur J. Van Alstyne. Plate 8, photo courtesy of Olivier Laude. Fig. 1.1, Xi'an Banpo Bowuguan (Banpo Museum, Xi'an), *Neolithic Site at Banpo Near Xian*, 1982 (in Chinese). Fig. 1.2, Guangzhou Shi Wenwu Guanli Weiyuanhui (Guangzhou Municipal Cultural Relics Administration), eds., *Han Dynasty Pottery Houses Excavated in Guangzhou*, 1958 (in Chinese). Fig. 1.3, adapted from *Xinhua zidian* (New Chinese Dictionary), 1984 (in Chinese). Fig. 1.4, redrawn from *Liaowang* (Outlook), 20 January 1986 (in Chinese). Fig. 1.5, *Jianzhu xuebao* (Architectural journal), 1962 (in Chinese). Fig. 1.6, Liu Dunzhen *Zhongguo zhuzhai gaishuo* (Introduction to Chinese Dwellings), 1957 (in Chinese). Figs. 1.7 and 1.8, drawings courtesy of the late Paul Sun, A.I.A. Fig. 1.11, photograph courtesy of Huang Hanmin. Fig. 2.1, drawing courtesy of Shen Dongqi. Fig. 2.3, *Er Ya* (Literary Expositor), *c*.4th century (in Chinese). Fig. 2.6, *Lu Ban yingzao zhengshi* (Correct Building Methods of Lu Ban), *c*.1368–1644 (in Chinese). Fig. 3.1, *Qinding Shujing tushuo* (Imperial illustrated edition of the *Historical Classic*), 1905 (in Chinese). Figs. 3.2 and 3.5, *Huitu Lu Ban jing* (Illustrated Manual of

Lu Ban), reprint edition 1987 (in Chinese). Fig. 4.1, Zhongguo jianzhu kexueyuan (Institute of Chinese Architectural Science), *Selection of Outstanding Proposals from the 1981 National Rural Housing Design Competition*, 1982.

Introduction

MORE than mere shelter, more than simply a vessel for daily life, the common Chinese house reflects a tradition of craft and symbolism that echoes that of China's great monumental architecture which produced well-known grand palaces, imperial graves, and walled cities. Both the folk and literate cultures communicate a dynamic tradition, revealing Chinese cosmology and beliefs in concrete and practical terms. Chinese buildings have a striking continuity of form. Unlike the cities and countryside of the West which may be read as museums of changing architectural styles, the cultural landscapes of China are remarkably ahistorical.

Archaeological and textual evidence reveals that late-imperial housing forms echo back to neolithic archetypes. Principles of symmetry, axiality, orientation, layout, and structure that took form millennia ago have recurred century after century down to the present. Two distinct antecedents of later architectural patterns emerged from the neolithic environments in the middle reaches of the Huanghe (Yellow River) and the wooded lower reaches of the Changjiang (Yangzi River).

Chinese archaeologists have postulated that in north China, domestic architecture began with rudimentary caves, evolving to semi-subterranean pit dwellings, then finally to surface dwellings with post-and-beam construction. The reconstructions of dwellings at the Banpo neolithic site near Xi'an in Shaanxi province, dated c.6,000 BC, give evidence of this progression, revealing clearly the formation by that time of a prototype.

Neolithic sites in the lower and middle reaches of the Changjiang in southern China have provided evidence of dwellings raised on wooden pilings. At the Hemudu site in Zhejiang province, dating from 7,000 BC, which includes the earliest evidence of cultivated rice in China, elaborate mortise and tenon joinery was discovered. Such ancient joining techniques used to notch or mortise pillars holding beams are widely practised today throughout much of the area south of the Changjiang.

Over time, what changes have occurred have been more incremental than radical, with a formidable 'strength of precedent', as it has been termed by Fernand Braudel. Infrequently, as with advances in tile and brick-making during the second millenium AD and more recent uses of pre-stressed concrete, innovative technologies have interrupted conservative building norms. But for the most part, one may look at a twentieth-century rural dwelling and see one of an earlier time.

Yet, Chinese dwellings are not uniform or stereotyped. Although there is a remarkable continuity of form and layout, common Chinese rural dwellings none the less display a regional diversity and a striking sensitivity to local environmental conditions. The extent of China's territory and the variety of natural environments offer partial explanations for these differences. During the sweep of Chinese history, continuing migration into diverse environments challenged settlers. Acutely conscious of the natural environment, builders have sensitively adapted inherited building forms to local requirements of site, available materials, and changing social circumstances. Such adaptations have not created new forms divorced from their ancestral precursors, but have ensured that their common heritage is preserved.

Experience, practicality, and economy have guided

Chinese housing form just as local conditions have governed building materials. An axiomatic element of well-developed Chinese houses is the wooden superstructure which not only supports the roof but also gives many Chinese roofs a distinctive shape. The use of wooden framework systems, composed of fitted pieces, has meant that the construction of Chinese buildings is but the fitting of one module to another. Used early in China, such load-bearing frameworks made it possible to separate support from enclosure, anticipating by many centuries curtain-wall skyscraper construction in the West.

Chinese folk traditions and the centrality of the family are revealed clearly in the Chinese house. The division and arrangement of space models the family relationships found within the dwelling, both in terms of ideals and practicality. The symbolism of house form and ornamentation evokes connections with many other aspects of Chinese culture, imitating in multiple 'little traditions' the cosmological predilections of 'the great tradition'. House-building is infused with practices that confirm the concern of the inhabitants for prosperity and happiness as well as protection against misfortune.

A striking building boom has been taking place in China over the past decade. Making up for years of deprivation, households throughout the country have been improving their dwellings through renovation as well as unparalleled new construction. Most new construction in China today clearly draws on traditional designs and practices. Some buildings however represent clear breaks with tradition, while fewer evidence truly revolutionary design innovations. Casual observers often express concern that all too much of the past is being destroyed in China's frenzied race towards modernization. Certainly, many grey and sterile multi-storied dwellings have been constructed in recent years through-out the country. Yet steps are being taken to design new dwellings that evoke China's rich architectural and folk traditions while at the same time providing environments with more space, air, light, and better sanitation.

I

The North and the South

COMMON and distinctive elements characterize Chinese building plans whether humble dwellings, palaces, or temples from earliest times to the present day. Regional and even local environmental, historical, or ethnic conditions have bequeathed patterns of striking diversity, however, these are insufficient to mask the common tradition. This apparent diversity includes not only rectangular shapes but also round and U- or H-shaped designs. For example, cave dwellings are a unique housing form which provide housing for some 40 million Chinese today in the loessial uplands in the middle reaches of the Huanghe (Yellow River). The multi-storied circular complexes found in Fujian and Guangdong provinces in south-east China peculiar to a Han ethnic subgroup, the Hakka or Kejia, are also unique. Further, the dwellings of the 55 ethnic minority groups which people China's periphery multiply the rich architectural mosaic of the country.

China has a long and continuing history, reaching back to neolithic times, of siting dwellings in optimal relation to the sun. A fundamental axial alignment for a dwelling is from east to west and facing south. This is underscored by the fact that the Chinese character for ridgepole (棟) is composed of elements for 'east' and 'wood', denoting that the principal wooden component of the roof is pointed east. Because the sun is regular in its path across the sky, the proper alignment of a house can control the degree to which the heat of the sun is seasonally captured or evaded. Moreover, there is a remarkable regularity to

Fig. 1.1 A precursor of later Chinese dwellings, this is a reconstruction of a neolithic dwelling at the Banpo site, Shaanxi province. A southern exposure, and overhanging eaves, as well as balance and axiality, prefigured later norms.

Fig. 1.2 Funerary pottery models of the Han period represent well-developed rural dwellings. The south-facing U-shaped dwelling depicted here was of two storeys. The upper floor served as living space, and the courtyard and lower floor were for livestock and other uses. Guangdong province.

summer winds from the south-east in most parts of the country, which is reflected in the orientation of dwellings. This overall environmental awareness was given the sanction of cosmological authority through the mystical ecology of *fengshui*, a subject discussed in a later chapter. Climate, thus, is an important form-generating factor in the construction of Chinese dwellings.

Northern Houses

Rectangular shaped rural houses are ubiquitous throughout northern China. The shape and organization of these houses reveal an early and continuing understanding of ways to overcome climatic problems. North China is a region of continental climate in which there is great disparity between winter and summer temperatures, with ranges usually exceeding 30°C. Rainfall is generally below 500 millimetres and is concentrated mostly in the three months of summer. Dry winter winds together with spring dust storms pummel much of the region from the north and north-west for more than six months of each year. In an environment in which timber is limited, peasants here have traditionally looked to the soil as their principal building material.

At its simplest, the typical north Chinese rural dwelling is a small one-storey rectangle with a depth of only a single room that responds well to these rather regular climatic conditions, using minimum resources to enhance physical comfort. Because the walls of dwellings are of pounded earth or adobe bricks, eaves are made to reach out sufficiently to retard rain wash of the walls. Furthermore, the slope of the roof is adjusted to a steeper pitch where rainfall is greater, with flat or nearly flat roofs where it is less. The ridgepole of most houses is arranged in an east–west direction. Accordingly, the façade is then oriented so that the door and windows face south, canonical considerations typical as well of Chinese temples and palaces that create satisfactory passive solar conditions and are evidence of striking climatic adaptation.

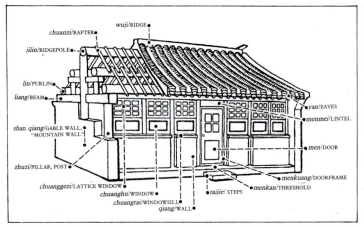

Fig. 1.3 Rectangular three-bay (*jian*) single-storey dwellings with windows only on the façade are ubiquitous in northern China. As shown in this figure, the central bay is fronted by a door and symmetrical windows, and each flanking bay has two window panels.

From earliest times, house builders throughout north China were concerned with securing heat from the sun in winter yet limiting it in summer as well as maximizing natural light throughout the year. This was accomplished by building one-storey rectangles facing south, by employing large windows across the façade, and by adjusting eaves-overhang to a depth related to the latitude of the location. The figure below shows that in the weeks surrounding the winter solstice when the noon sun angle is lowest, the sun's rays are able to pentrate deep into the dwelling through the expansive windows on the façade.

On the other hand, around the June solstice when the sun is high in the sky, the eaves-overhang effectively prevents the hot rays from entering the dwelling.

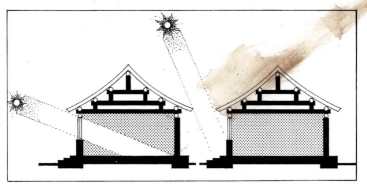

Fig. 1.4 Taking advantage of the regular path of the sun across the sky, Chinese builders adjusted the eaves and windows on the façade to block the high rays of the summer sun, but permit those of the low sun in winter to enter and warm the dwelling.

Northern houses generally have no windows on the west, north, or eastern sides and are often flanked on the rear by hills or other dwellings to militate against the steady winter and spring winds from these directions.

Known colloquially as the 'one bright, two dark' type, such dwellings typically contain three bays (*jian*) with a central room separating two bedrooms. The central room is the 'bright' room which opens to the outside through a middle door. Traditionally it has been the largest and highest room in a house. Here, at a location facing the main door a table is placed to hold ancestral tablets and the paraphernalia of ceremony. This room also serves as a place to store farm implements that cannot be left outside. In opposition, the adjoining 'dark' or interior rooms have always served as sleeping rooms and rooms for daily activities. Throughout north China, the central room is

9

also the location for at least one low brick stove, serving not only cooking needs but providing the heat in winter for the dwelling. The central stove has symbolic importance in the household since it signifies family unity.

Dominating each of the adjacent bedrooms is normally a *kang*, an elevated platform made of earthen bricks which in winter becomes a heat-dissipating surface for the hot air which passes from the nearby cooking stoves through a warren of flues embedded within each *kang*. For this reason and the fact that the *kang* absorbs the sun's rays which pass through the south-facing windows, the warmest spot in a house during the coldest times of the year is the *kang*.

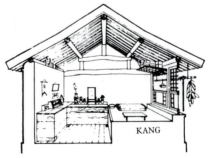

Fig. 1.5 An elevated brick platform called a *kang* is a common feature just inside the south wall of northern Chinese dwellings. During the winter the *kang* becomes a heat-dissipating surface, as hot air from a nearby stove is drawn through it.

By custom, the eastern bedroom is given to the senior generation, where it serves much of the year as a centre of family life. The elevated *kang*, even in summer, is a bright and surprisingly cool place for domestic chores such as sewing and food preparation. Because it is rarely unoccupied, the room is often used to store the more valuable articles of the household. The opposite bedroom is used by other members of the family, including usually a married son, his wife, and children. Grain is often stored here too. Each room typically contains a wooden, pottery, or enamelled bucket so that the family need not use the outside privy at night.

Traditional free-standing northern houses generally present a spartan appearance, broken only by the colourful decoration of windows and doors. The area in front of the house, which may be open or surrounded by a courtyard, is often untidy and the site of a latrine, a well, a storage shed for wood or straw, and improvised pens for raising a few chickens, ducks, or a pig.

Where the household's circumstances and resources make it possible, the rectangular house may be expanded by the addition of extra bays to lengthen the dwelling. In some cases, new structures may be added that are transverse to the main body to produce an L- or U-shaped dwelling. With these additions, a clear courtyard is formed.

Courtyard Houses

The full flowering of Chinese architecture is epitomized by the northern courtyard style where the principles of axiality, balance, and symmetry are well developed and clearly represented. Illustrated in the figure is a classical courtyard, the *siheyuan*. In each, the overall composition

of the residential quadrangle shows an orientation towards the south, clear axiality, and balanced side-to-side
symmetry. Representing as much as 40 percent of the
total area, the central courtyard and associated open
spaces are generous portions of the overall dwelling and
are larger than any of the structures which together make
up the house. These inward-facing structures surrounding the courtyard are single storey with narrow verandas,
providing a covered circuit for movement about the
complex. Symmetrical placement of trees, walkways, and
gateways complement the balanced proportions of the
siheyuan itself. Seclusion is guaranteed by the surrounding
walls and gates.

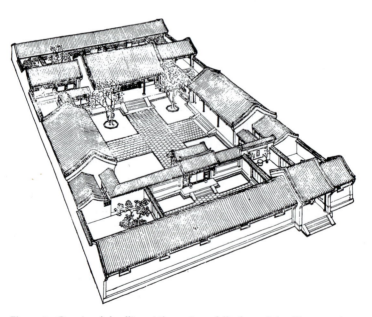

Fig. 1.6 Courtyard dwellings (*siheyuan*) are fully formed dwelling complexes
that epitomize Chinese domestic architecture, especially in the Beijing area of
northern China.

Seclusion as well as openness characterize these dwellings. From the street outside, a simple gate opens only to a shallow space that masks the scale of the dwelling within. The wrapping walls seclude the interior living environment from the external world. Each courtyard and building is situated in a pattern which defines hierarchy. Initial buildings and courtyards are the most public spaces and the most active, containing kitchens, store rooms, and rooms for servants.

The south-facing building fronting the larger courtyard is where the senior members of the family live, and has a layout very much like that of the common rectangular house of people of less means. Flanking the courtyard on the east and west are quarters for the families of married sons. From any place in the courtyard of these complexes, the sky appears to reach to distant horizons unobstructed either by parts of the dwelling or by neighbouring buildings. Outdoors and indoors flow together here to link the courtyard with adjacent living space, harmonizing the two and creating a private world for the residents. The *siheyuan* courtyard complexes echo on a small scale the plan of the imperial palaces.

Subterranean or Cave Housing

Throughout the ochre-coloured loessial uplands of north and north-west China, some forty million people live in dwellings dug into the living earth. Once covered with dense forests, this region is now semi-arid and has for millennia been overlain with thick layers of loess (wind-blown silt). Known in Chinese as 'yellow earth', loessial soils have given the Yellow River its characteristic colour and name. This region of easily tillable soil served also as a cradle of Chinese civilization.

Utilizing the abundantly available soil as a building material, farmers here have been able to construct dwellings that are remarkably cool in summer and warm in winter. In a region of continental climate with pronounced temperature extremes, this is evidence of a satisfactory adaptation. However, the infrequent but powerful earthquakes which assault the region have sometimes devastated these fragile structures, with substantial loss of life.

Two general types of cave or earth-sheltered dwelling can be seen throughout the region—cliffside dwellings and sunken courtyard caves. Both vary in size and complexity. Cliffside caves are dug into the steeply dissected loessial hill slopes and usually face south to benefit from the passage of the winter sun, as in other areas of north China. Sunken courtyard caves have been built in many areas of the mesa-like loessial plateau where cliffs are not available. Although subterranean, these dwellings retain orthodox characteristics of surface housing.

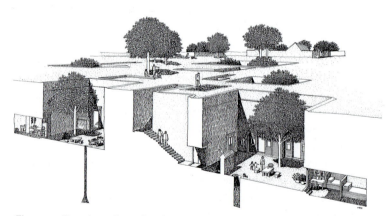

Fig. 1.7 Dug into the ochre loessial uplands which straddle the middle reaches of the Yellow River, cave-like dwellings provide housing today for some 40 million Chinese. Henan province.

The chambers which comprise cliffside dwellings have sides which usually rise some two metres from the floor before arching. The arches may be elliptical, semi-circular, parabolic, flat, or even nearly pointed. In height they are rarely more than five metres, with a depth of 10 to 20 metres. The width depends largely on the calcareous content of the soil. It is possible to span distances to a maximum of five metres where there is greater cohesion to the loess because of the increased lime content. Farmers have generally avoided damp soil found in the lower reaches of a gully, choosing instead a high location. This necessitates a long trek each day for water. Dug with simple tools, the subterranean dwelling takes upwards of three months to dry out completely. The walls are often coated with a plaster of loess or loess and lime to slow the drying and flaking of the interior. Sometimes bricks or stones are stacked to provide additional structural support.

A cave about six metres deep, three metres high, and three metres wide takes about forty days to excavate and prepare for initial occupancy. Properly maintained, most subterranean or earth-sheltered dwellings may be used for several generations. Where possible, a small amount of precious wood is used to give shape to the door and windows in the façade which is basically made of tamped earth or adobe bricks. Sometimes a false arch is sculpted above the actual opening to suggest greater exterior height.

In areas of the loessial plateau, farmers dig large rectangular pits which may exceed 100 square metres in size to form sunken courtyards. Often square and oriented towards the cardinal points of the compass, the sidewalls of these sunken courtyards provide surfaces into which caves can be excavated that are similar to the common cliffside dwellings just discussed. However, here it is possible to construct a residential complex that can accommodate a large extended family or even a hamlet of unrelated families. The sunken courtyard in many ways becomes a secure 'walled' compound and an important outdoor living space whenever the weather permits. Since it is open to the sky, rain or snow as well as dirt and dust fall or blow into the courtyard. Sometimes a low parapet is laid along the top as a ridge to impede the flow of water over the lip into the courtyard below.

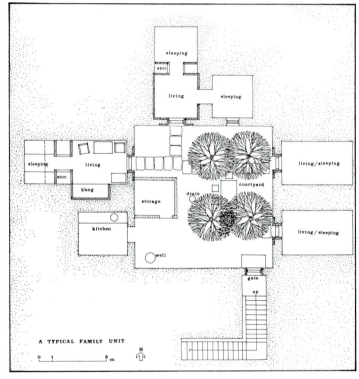

Fig. 1.8 The plan view of a sunken courtyard

The main chambers are usually on the north side of the sunken courtyard facing south, just as with common surface dwellings. Although chambers may be dug on the east and west sides, no caves are usually dug on the southern rim because this side is always in shade, even in summer. Within these complexes, some chambers may be connected. Shallow alcoves are commonly dug for storage space. Stairs, a ramp, or both are usually cut into the soil from the south to provide access to the level land above which is used for planting and for drying crops. In some areas of the loessial uplands, a village of subterranean housing may leave a landscape pocked with the deep indentations of courtyards.

Southern Houses

Covering more than half the area within the Great Wall, south China encompasses a variety of climatic conditions and landscapes that stretch southward from the valley of the Yangzi River. The fragmented topography of much of the south fostered the development of local traditions and nurtured local variations in many aspects of culture, including housing. This is as true in those areas of the southern border where Han Chinese intermingle with ethnic minority groups as it is where the population is clearly Han, such as in Zhejiang, Fujian, Guangdong, Hunan, and Sichuan.

Generally southern China is an area in which Han pioneers reclaimed virgin lands, bringing the basic rectangular northern housing-form to the region. In some cases, they adapted housing patterns of indigenous tribes even as they displaced them from the lowlands and pushed them into the highlands. Although primitive Chinese neolithic settlements in Zhejiang province show evidence of dwellings built on wooden pilings, later Chinese settlers never seem to have preferred houses built above ground level, although these are commonly found today in Japan and throughout South-east Asia.

Similar siting patterns to those found in North China also prevail in southern China. This preference for southern or south-eastern orientation however arises from a different set of climatic concerns.

In the south, where there is a much longer summer season and a relatively warm winter, it is necessary to foil the penetration of the sun by using few windows, together with thick white walls. In the north, dwelling façades provide passive solar conditions because of extensive windows on the southern side, whereas only a few small high windows are typically found in the traditional dwellings of the south, to block the direct rays of the sun and also reduce ground radiation.

Built to keep direct sunlight from reaching the interior, southern dwellings frequently exceed five metres in

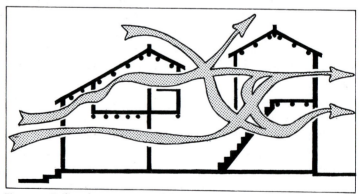

Fig. 1.9 Foiling the penetration of the sun as well as enhancing ventilation are important requirements of southern dwellings. These purposes are accomplished by limiting exterior windows to small high openings and building skywells which lead ambient breezes into the dark interiors.

depth. This is approximately twice the depth of northern dwellings where the low angle of the winter sun is able to penetrate deep into the room. Overhanging eaves as well as caps over windows and doors further block some of the heat-bearing rays of the summer sun. To accentuate this effect, thick walls of pounded earth or a mixture of composite materials act to insulate common dwellings from summer heat.

The walls of many southern dwellings are painted with a white lime plaster which serves to reflect rather than absorb solar energy. The overall compact plan of these dwellings further minimizes the surface area exposed to the sun, and results in a thermally efficient building mass. Deciduous trees are rarely used to shade the façade of such houses, contrary to the practice found in many areas of the world, largely because of the proscriptions of *feng-shui*. Shade from nearby dwellings generally contributes to mutual cooling, however. Detached kitchens also remove heat sources from living spaces in some houses.

Coupled with generally high subtropical temperatures is a seasonal precipitation pattern that brings more than 65 percent of the rain each year between April and September. Ample annual totals generally exceed 1,500 millimetres, at least triple the amounts found in northern China.

A particularly striking characteristic of the annual precipitation pattern in the lower Yangzi area are the so-called plum rains which arrive when the plum crop ripens, bringing about a month of overcast skies, intermittent drizzle, and showers during late May and June each year. Typical southern Chinese dwellings are built with steeply pitched roofs at an angle of at least 30 degrees in response to heavy summer rainfalls. Thatch roofs which quickly shed water were common in many poorer areas of the south in the past, although fewer are seen today. More common are roofs of baked tiles, laid so that there is a generous eaves overhang to shelter the walls from deterioration due to rain damage. Gable walls are generally capped with tile copings as a protective measure as well.

Fig. 1.10 Southern dwellings are commonly at least twice the depth of northern ones and are often quite compact, with thick insulating walls painted with a reflecting white plaster. Jiangsu province.

With these temperature and precipitation patterns comes relative humidity, usually at least 80 per cent in both summer and winter. Relative humidity is also highest during the plum rains, which are also called 'mould rains', using a Chinese homonym, because of the propensity of household items to mildew at this time of little sunlight and high humidity. Because of this fact, few items are stored directly on the cooler ground floor within southern houses. Instead, they are hung from pegs on the wall, suspended on hooks from the ceiling, piled on shelves, or stored in a loft.

To reduce mould formation and the rotting of wood as well as to mitigate the muggy conditions that contribute to discomfort and stress, a great deal of attention is paid to ventilation of southern dwellings. High walls with very few windows, it would appear, would frustrate such ventilation attempts. A southward or south-eastward orientation however facilitates receipt of the remarkably steady wind patterns experienced in coastal China in summer.

Ventilation in dwellings along the south-eastern coast is facilitated by the use of skywells and verandas. Sky-wells are sunken spaces which form an open shaft to capture ambient breezes and bring them into the dwelling. In some homes of the wealthy, they may reach ten

Fig. 1.11 Narrow skywells and broad eaves form verandas that open the interior of southern dwellings to light, and air, and provide a catchment area for rain-water. Fujian province.

metres and approximate actual courtyards, but most are much smaller. In addition to these large open areas, substantial eave overhangs limit direct sunlight from entering any of the rooms.

Verandas or arcades are transitional spaces between enclosed rooms and the open spaces of skywells and courtyards. The deep overhangs of the veranda, screen adjacent rooms from the harsh subtropical sunlight and prevent blowing rain from entering the living spaces. Thus, ventilation of the dwelling is made possible even under the worst weather conditions. Verandas permit inside activities to spill over to the outside and the outdoors to be immediately visible from the inside. They serve as covered corridors for people to move about the complex and as a place to sit halfway between indoors and outdoors in all weathers. Open-work lattice windows, often detachable, lead air into the rooms and serve a striking decorative purpose as well. Movable partitions frequently divide the inner space of southern dwellings, to heighten air circulation.

Although the small houses in both north and south China are simple rectangles that express the enduring penury of peasant life, the homes of the wealthy are strikingly different. Some of the characteristics of these dwellings reveal environmental and social conditions. A great deal of variation from area to area has resulted, reflecting not only differences in topography and economy but also the degree to which pioneers adopted local non-Chinese housing forms. Han pioneers encountered throughout the south a broader range of building materials available to them than in the north. Not only was timber more readily accessible, the grass bamboo was so widely distributed and found in such variety that it offered new possibilities.

Protective walls are common features of southern dwellings for both rich and poor. The need for protection arose out of building in remote hilly areas where bandits were common and where ethnic strife pitted one dialect group against another.

In Zhejiang, Anhui, Fujian, Jiangxi provinces, and near-by areas, compact two-storey dwellings are common. Appearing as inviolate ramparts, these dwellings are usually symmetrical in front elevation. They are generally entered through a door in the centre of a wall. Except for a pair of high windows, no other fenestration breaks any of the encircling walls. With white plaster walls and capped by grey brick roofs, these solid dwellings present a visually striking architectural contrast of line and colour.

Space within these dwellings is compact, yet arranged hierarchically as it is in full-form dwellings in the north. Instead of receding in depth as the courtyard or *siheyuan*-style dwelling does, these residences rise to provide privacy on the second storey.

Courtyards *per se* are not a feature of such dwellings, largely because of the scarcity of land. Instead, the narrow open spaces known as skywells or lightwells puncture the dwelling providing open shafts to catch the passing air and let light penetrate into the dwelling. In large residences with multiple skywells, each is usually proportionally smaller than surrounding rooms, serving principally to let in moving air and evacuate warmer air from the interior. In addition, the main central room on the ground floor is frequently fully open, shaded only by a broad veranda. Together, skywells and open rooms unite the indoors and the outdoors, creating an intermediate space and a living environment peculiarly characteristic of southern China.

A uniquely distinctive dwelling type is found in the

south-western sections of Fujian and adjacent portions of Guangdong province. Here, in an area of ethnic diversity, villages are usually compact and often composed of people with a single surname. The settlements of the Hakka, a Han Chinese ethnic sub-group which migrated into the region from central China, are striking because of their scale and shape. Known for their clannishness and unwelcomed to the point of hostility by other Chinese settlers who preceded them, the Hakka built their dwelling complexes in marginal hilly areas.

Whether the layout was square, rectangular, or round, these multi-storied complexes provided security. Whatever the shape, each dwelling has an axis and is essentially symmetrical. The lower floors serve utilitarian purposes, including space for kitchens, livestock, and storage. The number of stoves reveals the number of related households in the complex. At the centre is a prominent courtyard and hall for guests and for ceremonial purposes. Sometimes the courtyard is left open, the 'centre hall' being placed within the structure directly across the courtyard from the entrance. The second floor is used exclusively for the secure storage of grain and other food stocks.

Within these Hakka dwellings, the upper storeys are reserved for sleeping and generally have windows for ventilation and observation. Balconies ring these rooms and overlook the central courtyard. Giving the appearance of a fortification, each complex indicates the ethnic isolation of the Hakka.

In the south-western areas of the country, one encounters a cultural landscape of great variety. In the province of Sichuan which has a population exceeding one hundred million and is the size of Texas, no single generalization can express adequately the variety of dwelling types.

Here most of the population lives in smaller settlements, often isolated farmsteads or small hamlets. Rectangular dwellings are common, although they are usually capped by roofs of thick thatching or tile to shed the heavy rainfalls. Utilizing bamboo and timber from the well-forested hill lands, frame structures are quite common.

Whether a dwelling is a simple rectangle, is L- or U-shaped, or has an enclosed courtyard, is related to the resources of each rural household. In contrast with dwellings located in the north or even in south-eastern China, dwellings here are not strictly sited facing south or south-east, but are built with local topographic and microclimatic conditions in mind. Although the plans of small houses mimic those elsewhere in China, such houses rarely have windows on the façade and almost always have a broad overhang which shades the interior.

Sharing common building traditions with Chinese palaces and temples, rural houses reflect adaptations to local environmental and social conditions. In a nation which has nearly 10,000,000 square kilometres of land, Chinese farmers have shown sensitivity to diverse conditions. Although Chinese architecture—both on the small and the grand scale—emphasizes the horizontal, some dwellings in the south rise to several storeys. There is an additive quality to most dwellings, guided by notions of hierarchy and symmetry, that gives spatial definition to the changing human relationships contained within the dwelling.

2

Craft: Techniques and Materials

RURAL dwellings have largely been constructed by means of the accumulated experience of villagers themselves, supplemented when necessary by local carpenters and masons. Utilizing common structural components made of wood, earth, and stone in standard measurements, peasant builders and craftsmen have practised trades in which empiricism based upon economy and speed have been paramount.

Jian: a Building Module

The size and shape of inhabited space are guided by the structure of the dwelling as well as by utilitarian needs. In China the space between four columns, known as the *jian* or bay, 'the space between' is the common denominator, the unit of space manipulated as a module to give shape to all Chinese buildings. This space is both a two-dimensional floor space and also a volumetric measure of the void defined by the floor, the columns, and the beams set across the columns.

When linked with other *jian*, a geometrical grid is created which reveals the basic layout and scale of a structure. Ultimately, even the three-dimensional proportions of the dwelling derive from the size of the *jian* utilized, because of the interrelationships of specific building ratios. No less than in the construction of China's grand palaces and temples, the *jian* ultimately regulates the overall size of common dwellings and fashions their visual proportions.

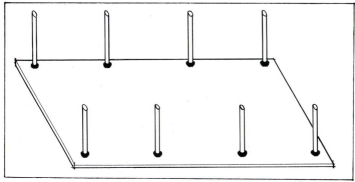

Fig. 2.1   The *jian* or bay, the interval between four columns, is the basic building module of a Chinese dwelling. Depicted here is the plan for a three-bay structure.

The smallest Chinese dwelling is composed of a single *jian*, a nucleus of habitation that provides flexible use of a common space for living, cooking, sleeping, and other activities. Space is expandable by adding pairs of parallel columns and extending the overhead roof purlins. Most Chinese dwellings are of three or five *jian*, linked laterally to form a line which is transverse to what is considered the axis of the house.

During the Qing period (1644–1911), imperial sumptuary regulations stipulated that the houses of common people could not exceed three *jian*, houses of officials seven, temples nine, and palaces 11. To the Chinese, odd numbers bring balance and symmetry to a dwelling and are considered lucky numbers. Houses with four or six *jian* are rare since they represent inauspicious and asymmetric shapes. The number four (*si*) is especially avoided since it is a homonym for the word 'death'.

The width and depth of the *jian* not only vary from place to place in the country but also differ according to the intended grandeur or simplicity of the dwelling. This is because the intercolumnar spacing governs the kind and quality of the wood to be used in the structural columns as well as the spanning beams which directly support the roof. A narrow spacing reduces the forces to be collected and transmitted to the ground by the vertical columns, thus permitting the use of smaller timber than where spacing is greater. Throughout China, the width of *jian* range between three and five metres. In northern China, the depth of a *jian* is usually similar to the width but in southern China the depth is double and sometimes even triple that found in the north.

The *jian* is thus a measurement used by carpenters as well as a structural unit, a design module to be duplicated in series to form the overall layout at ground level and on the floors above. Its use enforces a discipline, an order, on the building, standardizing the timber construction members and facilitating their assembly. Unwritten rules, often simply developed out of pragmatic considerations, traditionally determined proportions as well as the placement of ornamental details. Where the building site is not level because of terrain, adjacent *jian* can be on different planes yet be tied to the same rectilinear axis in a linked geometrical pattern. Using this repertoire of standardized elements, builders can even erect a complex dwelling by following the specification of a *jian* size, without the guidance of drawings.

Foundations

Throughout China, buildings are constructed without basements. Following building traditions which reach back at least as far as the Shang dynasty (roughly 1600–1100 BC), a tamped earth foundation or podium at ground level or only slightly elevated is considered the necessary base. Coupled with troughs and sometimes underground conduits to drain water, tamped foundations provide a dry foundation for a dwelling. Chinese migrants continued this predilection for construction directly on the ground, utilizing it even where its appropriateness was questionable and where indigenous tradition offered an alternative—not only in areas of southern China but throughout peninsular South-east Asia where raised dwellings on piles reduced humidity by ventilation from beneath. Chinese archaeologists have discovered that primitive Chinese residents of Hemudu in eastern Zhejiang province constructed raised dwellings on piles about 7,000 years ago, but the practice was abandoned. This tradition is not observable in any contemporary dwellings of the Han Chinese, although such raised dwellings are inhabited by many ethnic minority groups in the south.

In an effort to reduce the absorption of soil moisture by the walls, stone foundations or wall footings are commonly laid along the tamped perimeter of Chinese dwellings. This stone base is sometimes extended beyond the wall line to further mitigate the flow of water from the roof, and is raised above ground level to protect the lower wall from water damage. Splashing of water which has flowed from the roof or from driving rain would otherwise, over time, substantially wear away the vulnerable lower walls of most dwellings. Below ground the rough cut stone is usually packed tightly following its natural shape and held without mortar, while mortar is used with elevated bases. In none of these cases is it the function of the structural underpinnings to fasten the structure to the ground. Instead they simply stabilize the base and isolate the damp ground from the structure above.

Fundamentals of Chinese Structures

Chinese builders span and enclose space using a variety of solutions to collect the forces of gravity and transmit them to the ground. These structural solutions are distinguished principally in terms of whether the walls are load-bearing or not. Solid, load-bearing walls which directly carry the weight of upper storeys are common throughout rural China today as they always have been because of the penury of the rural population. Better known, however, are the structural systems based upon wooden frameworks that sustain the load of upper storeys and the roof independently of the walls. These wooden frameworks predominate in the architecture of Chinese palaces and temples, but are found as well in higher quality residences throughout the countryside. Much as in contemporary skyscraper construction, this unique structural solution is one in which walls are mere curtains while the weight is carried by the structural framework. Erected as a free-standing skeleton in anticipation of the raising of the surrounding walls, this innovation has made possible the flexible treatment of interior space, utilizing free-standing lightweight interior walls separate from the load-bearing columns.

Walls

Walls may either be load-bearing or non-load-bearing. Load-bearing walls which directly support the roof structure, are often thick with few breaks for windows or doors. Where wooden skeletal frameworks are used, non-load-bearing walls may encircle the framework or be placed between the pillars. In both cases, common materials are used: tamped earth or a composite material, adobe or kiln-dried brick, wood, grasses, and stone. With wooden frameworks, bamboo matting, wattle and daub may be used as well to form the curtained enclosure of poorer dwellings.

Fig. 2.2 Load-bearing walls of tamped earth, adobe brick, stone, or, as shown here, fired brick are often used to support the roof directly. Because of the width of this dwelling, an interior wooden framework is used as well. Guangxi Zhuang autonomous region.

Tamping or pounding earth into solid walls, the *hangtu* method of construction, has been used throughout Chinese history in virtually every province, as a building method suitable in times of scarcity for anyone having access to soil. Using a wide range of common soil types, the method has been used not only for the walls of houses and other buildings but in the construction of fortifications and other defensive works such as city walls and the Great Wall. Known in the West as *pise de terre*, this technique involves piling freshly dug earth into a slightly battered caisson or box frame that is framed on its long sides by movable wooden poles or boards. In order to increase its bearing strength, the earth is then pounded with stone or wooden rammers until it is sufficiently firm to support the tamping of another layer above it. The movable shutters of the timber frame are then raised, levelled, clamped into place and the process repeated until the wall reaches the desired height. Once the frame is removed, the wall is left with a rough surface due to the impression of the frame; these depressions facilitate the application of a plaster surface if desired after the wall dries completely. In northern China, the surface is usually left to weather to a natural hue. Throughout south China, a white lime plaster is frequently added that serves not only as a protective coating against rain wash but also to reflect sunlight and keep the dwelling cool.

Fixed elongated removable frames are also commonly used in house construction today as in the past. Appearing as a three-sided box without a cover or bottom, such

Fig. 2.3 *Hangtu* or tamped earth construction is a traditional technique utilizing locally available soils to raise an inexpensive wall.

Fig. 2.4 Following traditional methods, fresh earth is added to a wooden frame, then pounded with a rammer to form a wall.

frames exceed one metre in length and 33 centimetres in height and width. They have wooden dowels to facilitate movement. A narrow end-piece is mortised through the long sides while the other end is temporarily held by a removable rectangular brace. The lower leg of the brace passes through the rising wall, and is compelled to grip the bottom flanks of the frame tightly, by the forcing of a wedge into the upper leg. Frames for a limited number of windows are placed in the wall as it rises, the number being kept small because of the need for the wall to carry the weight of both the upper wall and the roof. The impression of the box frame and wooden dowels on the walls of the completed house is usually quite apparent.

Modifications of the technique include mixing additional materials such as straw, paper, and oils with the clay-like soil to increase its binding capacity and strength.

In some areas of the south, walls are tamped using only a relatively small proportion of earth, depending upon larger amounts of sand and lime to form a composite type of mortar. A common mixture is 60 per cent sand, 30 per cent lime, and 10 per cent earth, producing walls of uncommon firmness akin to those formed using concrete. Usually a course or two of bricks or stone is finally added along the top of such walls to retard rotting of the roof purlins which may rest directly on or be embedded in the walls.

In addition to tamped earth walls, walls of adobe and kiln-dried brick are also used throughout China. Adobe bricks have been the materials used generally by poorer peasants, while fired bricks are preferred by those who can afford them. As with *hangtu*, bricks depend upon accessible soils available in every locale throughout the country. The widespread use of soil as a building material even in areas where wood is common reflects the widespread penury of the Chinese villagers and the need to conserve available wood for fuel for cooking and heating. Adobe bricks, while retaining the economic and technical advantages of tamped earth, permit greater variations in construction form and represent a tangible statement that a household is not as poor as its neighbour.

Bricks, whether they are sun-dried adobe or fired in a kiln, are made using a variety of methods that, as depicted in the seventeenth-century manual *Tiangong kaiwu* ('The creations of nature and man'), have not changed for centuries. Common adobe bricks are usually formed in non-releasable moulds into which earth is scooped, levelled by hand or by using a bow, and then left to air dry. The soil may be naturally moist or water may be added. Sometimes the earth in the mould is rammed with a pestle, much after the fashion of *hangtu* construction, to increase the compression of the brick. Bricks formed in this manner are usually produced in the autumn, after the second rice harvest, at a time that permits the bricks to cure slowly. Many such bricks are poorly compacted and thus prone to deterioration due to rain wash or flood.

Fig. 2.5 The method of brick making depicted in this seventeenth-century print can be observed all over China even today. The earth is packed into the wooden frame and a wire bow is used to cut off the excess before the bricks are left to dry in the sun.

Where the bricks are to be fired, greater care is taken in mixing the soil and water as well as in moulding. Extra attention is paid to natural drying. This normally takes a week before the bricks are placed in the kiln. Unlike adobe bricks, those prepared for firing can be made all the year round. The kilns are fired using coal, grain stalks, boughs of trees, or brush. The length of firing, the degree of heat, the addition of water as well as the original soil act to alter the texture and colour of the brick. Especially in southern China, the fired bricks are thin and usually laid in a box-bond pattern to form hollow walls. Walls made of fired bricks usually have larger and more numerous openings for windows and doors than is the case with tamped earth or adobe walls.

In some areas of southern China, bricks are cut directly from the base of irrigated rice fields where siltation has raised the level of the field. Approximately once every ten years, after the autumn harvest, the field is ploughed and harrowed. Once evaporation has reduced the moisture content of the soil to the consistency of putty, brick-size sections of soil are cut with a spade from the floor of the field. Pounded into a frame with the feet, the bricks are left to cure for several weeks.

Stone has not been used in China as a construction material to an extent that matches its availability, except in the building of graves where its indestructability, and capacity to keep moisture from entering the burial space made it the material of choice. Stone, however, is used to form the walls of houses throughout the extensive mountainous and coastal areas of the country where it is readily available and soil itself is thin. Cut into brick-like shapes, such stone walls provide an uncommonly strong support for a heavy roof and facilitate the placement of windows and doors in ways not possible with earthen bricks or tamped earth. Stone also serves as paving, support for pillars, and decorative embellishment.

Tamped earth and adobe brick walls constituted nearly 50 per cent of all farm buildings in China in the early 1930s, while fired brick represented another 20 per cent. The remaining 30 per cent were of vegetative origin, mainly of bamboo, *kaoliang*, or cornstalks that bear no load from above and form curtain walls. Common especially in central, south-eastern, and south-western China, these are all curtain walls set between pillars. Bamboo may be split, interlaced at a 90-degree angle, and plastered with mud or mud and lime to make a wall tight to air and moisture. Especially in the homes of the poor or in temporary shelters, a reed or finely split bamboo matting will be sufficient to screen the elements and provide a modicum of privacy. Whatever the walling on the side and back walls, the preferred material in much of China for the façade is solid or intricately carved panels of wood which serve less to enclose than other functional purposes and make possible a degree of ornamentation.

Wooden Structural Frameworks

An axiomatic element of Chinese monumental architecture that is found in dwellings as well is a wooden framework that rises from the ground to support the weight of the roof without the assistance of the walls. This wooden skeleton may be integrated into the wall and appear as part of the enclosure or it may be located inside, separate from the wall. Both types are found throughout China. No attempt is usually made to conceal the pillars or beams, the natural lines of which are considered a beautifying attribute to both the exterior and the interior. The use of a weight-bearing wooden superstructure makes possible an extraordinary flexibility in the placement of windows and doors in the encircling walls, with less concern for the weakening of walls.

Wooden framework structures are distinguished fundamentally by the means in which the various rising elements are interlocked to give shape to the roof. Two distinctive and traditional framing systems can be identified: pillars-and-beams (*tailiang* or *liangzhu*) and pillars-and-transverse tie beams (*chuandou*). The repertoire of the elements of these framing systems in house construction mimic the elaborations of temples and palaces.

The simplest pillar-and-beam frame (which may also be called a post-and-lintel frame) includes a pair of pillars supporting a horizontal beam upon which are set short

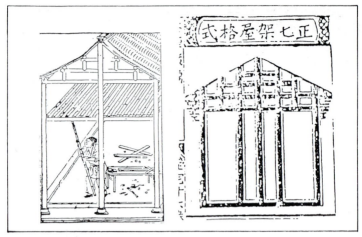

Fig. 2.6 Wooden skeletal frameworks which directly support the roof, as shown in carpenters' manuals. On the *left* is the *tailiang* ('pillars and beams') type and on the *right* is the *chuandou* ('pillars and transverse tie-beams') type.

vertical posts or struts to lift another beam, upon which is fitted another strut. On these are fitted five purlins which define the slope of the roof and across which the roof rafters are laid. This simple type is found throughout north China. The load of the roof is indirectly carried to the pillars by the horizontal beams which span the space between, providing the base upon which crosswise purlins, roof rafters, and roof tiles rest. Chinese builders traditionally believed that the sturdiness of a structure was ensured by placing great weight on it, hence the use of beams and purlins far heavier than would seem necessary to carry even the weight of unusually massive tile roofs.

The *chuandou* framing system, most common in southern China where dwellings are deeper than they are in the north, differs from the *tailiang* system in three important ways: the roof purlins which support the rafters and roof

Fig. 2.7 Pillars support massive horizontal beams upon which pairs of short struts rise to lift another beam on this *tailiang* ('pillars and beams') frame. Each beam directly supports the roof purlins as well as the weight of the rafters and roof tiles. Walls are thus mere curtains, enclosing rather than bearing a load. Beijing area.

itself rest directly on notched pillars rather than on beams or struts; the number of pillars is greater; and horizontal tie beam members are mortised directly into or tenoned through the multiple pillars to form an interlocked matrix that inhibits skewing of the frame. The weight of the roof is generally carried directly by each pillar to the ground, although in some cases short struts supporting purlins rest on horizontal tie beam members instead of being extended to the ground. (See colour plate 12.)

The great number of full length pillars and truncated pillars is necessitated by the fact that individually each pillar is weakened by the grooves or slots which are mortised to hold the horizontal tie beams. This weakening leads obviously to an increase in the number of pillars and a decrease in their spacing in comparison with the *tailiang* system in which none of the pillars is made less stable by cutting. By multiplying the vertical and horizontal members, the timber used may then be of smaller diameter, frequently only 20–30 centimetres and therefore less expensive than that used in *tailiang* frames. It is possible that this framing system developed in response to a shortage of building timber of sufficient size to construct dwellings according to the pillar-and-beam principles. In neither case are braces used to stabilize the frames.

With a *chuandou* matrix, one set of lateral tie beams is usually sufficient for a frame with three pillars reaching the ground, two sets for five, three sets for seven, and four for nine. It is possible to vary these rules depending on the quality of the available timber as well as other needs, for example, by adding short pillars resting on individual tie beams to support additional purlins or by inserting horizontal beams to support floor boards for a loft. By extending a tie beam beyond the façade of a dwelling, a cantilevered arm is created to support a projecting eave and eaves purlin without using a corbelled bracket set. Pegs of various shapes are utilized to hold beams with tenons in place as are wooden wedges to ensure a tight fit.

Elaborate, ingenious, and complex mortise and tenon systems involving very heavy wooden horizontal pieces are found in large dwellings, temples, and clan halls throughout China. Often slightly crescent-shaped, these are usually richly carved, rising rhythmically towards the exposed ceiling. The use of complex mortar and tenon systems has a long history in China, reaching back to the neolithic period.

The preferred location for a wood framing system is

1 Built of three *jian*, this simple single-storey dwelling in central Shanxi province is of a type found widely throughout the villages of northern China.

2 Arranged on three sides of a sunken courtyard dug into loessial soil, this subterranean dwelling remains warm in winter and cool in summer. Shaanxi province.

3 Similar to the rectangular dwellings of north China, but with a steeply pitched double-slope roof, this new brick dwelling in Sichuan province follows traditional patterns. Deep eaves along the front shade the dwelling and protect the walls from rain wash. They also provide covered exterior working space and an area to hang crops to dry.

4 Compact two-storey dwellings with white plaster walls and limited fenestration to keep direct sunlight from the interior. Southern China, Anhui province.

5 Built on an elevated stone foundation, the walls of this dwelling are of unplastered tamped earth. The holes indicate the location of the brace for the tamping frame. Zhejiang province.

6 Along the canals throughout the Jiangnan region of the lower Yangzi River, canal-side dwellings usually have overhanging verandas and a height which permits a loft. Zhejiang province.

7 Dwellings with an open central room are common in the south-eastern coastal areas of China. Such dwellings may be open to the street like this one, or hidden behind high walls.

8 Circular multi-storey communal residences, 'forts' of inexpensive tamped earth have been built for several centuries in south-western Fujian and north-eastern Guangdong provinces by the Hakka, a Han Chinese ethnic subgroup.

9 Skywells, which allow ambient air to ventilate the interior but keep most of the heat-bearing sunlight out, are common in southern dwellings. Zhejiang province.

10 Load-bearing walls of brick directly support the heavy wooden roof purlins as well as the rafters and roof tiles on this typical northern Chinese dwelling. Beijing northern rural county.

11 *Chuandou* wooden frameworks are used throughout central and southern China. As can be seen here, the roof purlins, rafters, and tiles are supported directly by the relatively light wooden framework, leaving space between to be filled with free-standing curtain walls. Sichuan province.

12   This *chuandou* frame exhibits the mortise-and-tenon joints which articulate it. On an auspicious date, the red cloth is hung in celebration of the raising of the ridgepole. Zhejiang province.

13 Blocks of silt are cut from the rice paddy floor, placed in bamboo frames, dried, and used as bricks. Guangxi Zhuang autonomous region, Southern China.

14 *Matou qiang* ('horse's head walls') are striking stepped gable walls which originated as fire walls to separate the wooden structures of adjacent buildings in compact villages. Anhui province.

15 On this partially completed dwelling, the sweeping profile of the roof mimics that of a swallow's tail. Cut stone forms the walls. Fujian province.

16 The central room of a Chinese dwelling has traditionally served ritual as well as secular purposes.

immediately inside an encircling brick wall, a common configuration found in homes of the wealthy or within a tamped wall of a more humble dwelling. The continuous bond of the encircling brick wall is a stronger enclosure than that provided by interval walls laid between individual pillars. A pillar, the vertical element of a wooden framework, normally sits on a stone plinth to protect the wood from dampness, and the encroachment of termites, as well as to distribute the load carried by the pillar to the base beneath. The plinth itself may rest either on bare pounded-earth or on a stone support. Plinths range from roughly hewn stone blocks to carved stone forms such as drums, octagons, squares, and lotus flowers.

Ground sills to tie the columns together at the base and steady the structure, such as those used in Japanese vernacular architecture, are not used with Chinese wood frames. Because pillars are not anchored to the ground or connected at their base, they are able to move easily with rather than against the tremors of earthquakes, common along China's eastern coast. This arrangement enables horizontal movements to be countered by flexibility, permitting a resonance to the overall structure. Although walls themselves might fall as a result of even a weak earthquake, the integrity of the costly wood framework most likely would be maintained and only the cheaper walls would need to be reconstructed.

Sometimes a pair of wooden frames, either *tailiang* or *chuandou*, are used in conjunction with load bearing walls, especially in long dwellings. The longitudinal purlins thus are seated high in the side walls and carried across the interior space to the wooden frames which define and support the middle bays of the building. The length of a dwelling depends on the number of front-to-back frames; its height is governed by the length of the pillars and the placement of the floor joists. A dwelling can be enlarged longitudinally by positioning a matching frame beyond the existing structure and adding additional purlins.

As a general rule, an increase in the depth of a dwelling is reflected in increasing height. Extending the depth from a single to a double bay augments the potentially usable space beneath the rafters by a factor of three, making possible the construction of lofts for secure and dry storage as well as for sleeping. Such ancillary lofts are set upon joists which have been notched into the frames. Depth is fixed by the number of purlins and the pitch of the roof. Rural houses in southern China are much deeper than those commonly found in north China. With purlins spaced one to one and a half metres apart, the depth sometimes reaches ten metres, allowing the interior space to be divided into front and back rooms, a layout rarely encountered in the north. Furthermore, extensions beyond the eaves can be added to form a veranda, supported by eaves or peripheral pillars, a common feature of southern dwellings.

Dwellings of two or three storeys can be constructed using either of these framing systems. In southern provinces, where there is limited level land, a folk saying refers to this as 'borrowing the sky instead of the land'. Even where terrain is uneven along stream banks or in the hills, a stepped dwelling may be built down a slope by utilizing a linked series of pillars and beams without compromising the integrity of the common framing systems.

The interdependence of the bay (*jian*) building module and the wooden framework standardizes traditional Chinese architecture to a remarkable degree. As related systems, the bay and the wooden framework permit a high degree of flexibility and freedom of design—

essential for rural dwellings that normally undergo altera-
tion and expansion as family size and fortune allow.
Equal heights of pairs of pillars, the equidistant spacing of
purlins and other building components simplify and
standardize the construction process, making possible a
surprising level of prefabrication and modularization.
Structurally, the number and spacing of purlins regulates
the length of rafters, stabilizing and equally distributing
the massive weight of most Chinese roofs. Standardiza-
tion based upon traditional principles of measurement has
survived up to the present day, now making possible the
economical fabrication of building members using new
materials such as concrete joists, purlins, and floor panels,
as well as other low cost mass-produced building
materials.

Roof Profiles

At first glance, the roof profiles of the *tailiang* and *chuandou* structures appear similar to those resulting from the
truss system used to define common Western roofs. Unlike the truss, which is based upon triangularly positioned
segments to carry the load, both Chinese systems, depend upon the pillars, struts, or beams to collect the
forces via the roof purlins and transfer them to the
ground. By altering the distance between purlins according to specific ratios, even pronounced curvature can be
introduced into the roof profile. Where a straight roof
line is not desired, rafters are cut into appropriate lengths
to reach from one purlin to the next, in order to break
slope and define the curvature of the roof. Clay roof tiles,
added piece by piece and embedded in a binding composition, can be arranged to heighten curvature. Rather
straight and less graceful rooflines are traditionally found

on humble dwellings while freer designs are found on residences of those with more means.

Roof profiles are normally symmetrical in side and front elevation, the first emphasizing the area where the roof meets the gable end and the second the line of the ridgepole. Four major roof profile types are common throughout China, with a fifth found only in the areas to the south of the Yangzi River. A mixture of styles is sometimes found in a single dwelling, indeed on a single roof. There are a greater variety of roofs in south China. These have more ornamentation and curvature than those in the north. Flat roofs are common only in the semi-arid areas of the north and west.

Throughout north and north-eastern China, the most common roof profile is the *yingshan ding* or 'firm mountain' type. This is especially suited to areas of limited rainfall where there is no need for overhanging eaves on the gabled end to protect the wall from weathering. This type is seen also in areas of substantial rainfall, for example the central and southern parts of the country where it is usually found with kiln-dried brick.

The 'overhanging gables' roof style (*xuanshan ding*) is usually combined with the use of overhanging eaves on the façade to offer a degree of protection from both rain and sun. Its utilization is especially common where the walls are made of wooden panels or slats and wattle and plaster. Hipped roofs and combined hip and gable wall roofs are especially common on Chinese palaces and temples. Prior to the Song dynasty, hipped roofs were apparently standard on Chinese dwellings as well, but subsequent sumptuary regulations imposed during the Ming and Qing dynasties officially restricted them to palaces.

Gable walls which rise above the roof line to create a

Fig. 2.8 The 'firm mountain' (*yingshan ding*) roof profile which is the most common in northern China. Shaanxi province.

striking ornamental and functional element are especially common in Anhui, Zhejiang, and adjacent areas in south central China. Termed 'horse's head walls' (*matou qiang*), this type of wall originated as fire walls to retard the spread of sweeping roof fires in adjacent dwellings, temples, clan halls, and other buildings in towns and nucleated villages. Sometimes they are found in an abbreviated form, appearing as a sweeping longhorn, added to extend a building's flush gable-wall forward to frame a front or rear courtyard; they are often accentuated with tile copings. Kiln-dried bricks covered with a plaster are generally used with these expensive walls so that the lack of an overhang on the solid wall is of little significance.

45

Fig. 2.9   Rhythmically rising stepped gables (*matou qiang*). Zhejiang province.

Roofing Materials

The function of a roof is to shelter the structure and its interior from the elements. Where rainfall is great, there is an obvious need to retard the infiltration of water, and lead it to the eaves where it will fall to the ground. The use of waterproofing materials and roof slopes make this possible. Insulation from cold or heat is frequently another concern of builders. To reduce the splashing of water as it drops to the ground, the roof line is generally extended by using broad eaves.

Until recent decades, dwellings with thatched roofs were numerous throughout the Chinese countryside, in the north as well as the south. They were common on the houses of the poor as well as on the rural residences of the literati who sought inspiration from a simple rural life.

46

Throughout north China, thatching has consisted mainly of wheat straw, *kaoliang* stalks, millet stalks, and reeds. Rice straw and wild grasses have commonly been used in southern China to provide a thatched roof that is relatively water-repellent. In some of the more remote upland areas, the bark of fir trees continues to be cut into concave sections and laid like split bamboo or concave tiles to lead water to the eaves. Where locally available, slate as well as shale provide reasonably impervious roofing material when overlapped in large sheets.

Half-burnt roof tiles, with local variations in shapes and patterns, have a long history in China. In the 1930s, in the prosperous rice and tea growing areas of the country, more than 80 per cent of dwellings had tile roofs of one type or another. The practices recorded in the seventeenth-century , manual *Tiangong kaiwu* ('The creations of nature and man'), are still encountered throughout China, drawing upon locally available soil resources. In some areas, tiles are set into a bonding layer of mud, but in much of the southern areas of the country, the weight of the tiles themselves provides stability. In such cases the tiles rest directly on a base layer formed either by the rafters or a reed matting. Periodically, especially after a windy storm, tiles must be realigned on the roof. Vertical rows of alternating and overlapping concave and convex tiles produce gutters which carry rain water quickly to the eaves. Decorative drip tiles are not found on the common houses but are added only to the homes of those who are better off.

Throughout the north China plain and in the northeast, roofs which are flat, curved, or with only a slight pitch are common. Most roofs of this type are layered compositions of mineral and vegetative materials. Varying from place to place, these generally include rafters upon which reeds or grain stalks either loose or formed into mats are laid as a base. Then, several layers of a mud and straw composition are tamped into place before being covered by additional layers of lime and mortar to seal the roof.

The roof in Chinese domestic and monumental architecture is often a striking visual element that not only ornaments but also expresses status. Unlike the roofs of palaces and temples, those of common dwellings in the north are rather rigid and plain. It is in the areas to the south of the Yangzi River, however, that the roof as the architectural high point is reached, with not only the upper gable serving as a surface for ornamentation but also the ridgeline itself. Stylized gable profiles may be enhanced with decorative additions that evoke symbolic meanings. In side elevation, as discussed above, the stepped and rising 'horse's head walls' of the Jiangnan area are especially striking in their simplicity. The symmetrical ridgelines of many dwellings in southern China often take a graceful curve, with the curvature accentuated by flying eaves at the ends to form sweeping 'swallow's tail' roof profiles. Common in Fujian, Taiwan, and parts of Guangdong, the upsweeping curvature of the swallow's tail style was modified from the 'owl's tail' of China's great architectural tradition. Officially restricted by sumptuary laws for use only in the construction of palaces, temples, official buildings and the residences of degree holders, this graceful style was adopted by builders on China's margins who could flout the regulations. Along the ridgelines of some of these dwellings, moulded mortar is embellished with porcelain fragments to suggest spirited animals, auspicious fruits, and other symbolic items.

Fig. 2.10 Large dwellings in Taiwan and in south-eastern China, frequently possess graceful and sweeping roof profiles, termed the 'swallow's tail' type (*yanwei xing*).

3

Symbol and Tradition

THE construction of a Chinese house has by tradition entailed more than the work of carpenters and masons applying their craft to shape materials and give form to space. House-building and house form throughout the country reveal family relations, and have been infused with folk practices that express Chinese cosmology and folk beliefs in practical terms. There are among the Chinese tenacious beliefs in the power of the supernatural to summon good fortune and guard against misfortune as a family attempts to ride out the phases and vicissitudes of life. It is not surprising that many of these beliefs centre about the building and occupancy of their homes. On the mainland and in Taiwan and Hong Hong even today, the resilience of these folk traditions is clearly observable in spite of rapid modernization.

Jia: *Home and Family*

A Chinese rural dwelling is a domain, a territorial unit set apart to function not only as living space for a family but often also as a place of gainful activity for the household. Commonplace and simple dwellings take many forms, varying to a greater degree than do either the different kinds of Chinese family or even their means of making a living. Each dwelling is a dynamic entity that expresses the organization, fortunes, status, and aspirations of those living within it. These factors may change as external and internal forces operate on the Chinese family guiding its passage from one form to another.

'*Jia*' is the Chinese word for both home the dwelling, and family, the related members of the household who occupy it. The *jia* shelters the household, providing it with a haven from the changing forces of nature. Yet the layout of a dwelling is more than that of a static vessel for daily life. The dwelling is symbolic of family unity and sanctuary, a public statement of status as well as a tangible expression of the family's aspirations. It is a dynamic entity that expresses in varying degrees the changing relationships within the family, symbolizing and accommodating evolving hierarchical patterns. The individual is essentially disregarded in the organization of the layout of a Chinese dwelling, with space defined more broadly in terms of family rather than personal needs and use. Little consideration is given to privacy, for individuals or even parents. Furthermore, no specific space is defined as the exclusive preserve either of men or of women.

Enclosure and separation are basic elements of Chinese architecture, whether expressed in the encircling wall of a capital city or that of a single dwelling. The wall circumscribes and detaches the internal world from that found without, providing seclusion and privacy for those behind it. In southern China where dwellings vary in height, houses have traditionally been built to isolate the residence both from neighbours and from the surrounding environment. Adjacent houses are generally of the same height so that no neighbour can peer into a nearby one. Whether built of thatch, tamped earth, or brick, southern houses rarely have more than token windows facing the outside, especially at ground level. Sometimes nothing breaks a wall except for a single doorway along the façade or a side, presenting an uninviting exterior meant to exclude. In other areas of China such as southern Fujian where Chinese pioneers pushed into frontier areas inhabited by indigenous groups, high thick walls of dwellings served to counter the fear of unsettled conditions as well as local banditry.

Within the enclosure which defines the dwelling, poorer people generally make more flexible use of space than do wealthier people. Within small dwellings of a single room, where the family is at an early stage of formation and fortune, living space is often shared with working space. Furniture, tools, and agricultural raw materials for processing frequently vie for the same space. As fortune permits, this small space may be extended by the addition of a room to each flanking side to form a rectangular dwelling, perhaps the most common form seen throughout the country. Where means permit, the dwelling itself may be comprised from the start of three rooms, defined as three *jian*. In either case, the central room becomes a common room with the side rooms bedrooms.

Throughout China, the common room or main hall at the centre serves ritual as well as secular purposes. It may be a simple room or be rather grand and lavishly decorated. Symbolic of continuity, this central room commonly contains a high, long table upon which ancestral tablets, images of gods and goddesses, as well as the paraphernalia of ceremony are arranged. Above the table, a large decorative print and a pair of vertical couplets are usually hung. Periodic offerings of food and incense acknowledge patrilineal descent and communal links. Often high, with exposed beams blackened by the burning of incense, the room usually has the dwelling's only door which serves to bring light into this space. However large the family and the dwelling become, this room is accepted as joint property never to be divided.

In most areas of the country, the sleeping room to the

left of the common room was traditionally reserved for parents and termed 'the great room'. Children would sleep in the room on the opposite side. Such an ordering recognized hierarchy, significance, and seniority which was further emphasized as additional rooms were added. Movement along the axis away from the common room was a passage from public space to private domain. With the courtyard houses of the wealthy, depth along a longitudinal axis represented a similar hierarchical pattern.

Among China's rural population, additional rooms have usually been arranged perpendicularly to the axis of the core rectangle. These connecting side buildings, first on the left and then on the right, served a growing family as bedrooms for younger members as well as storage or cooking space. Embraced between these flanking wings, a courtyard thus took form which gave the dwelling a U-shape that might be closed with a wall.

Under ideal conditions and where there was increasing wealth, the conjugal unit sometimes evolved to extended forms through the marriage of sons, but this was less common than is generally believed in the West. In these cases, as wealth and human relations allowed, the dwelling might grow in a lateral or forward direction. Farm households normally grew laterally with flanking wings while the domiciles of the wealthy sometimes stretched to great depth through the addition of new U-shaped units.

Anthropologists and novelists have revealed some of the reasons why the growth and expansion of dwellings did not occur with greater frequency. Tensions within families and the lack of primogeniture frequently forced the division of a family into smaller units of related nuclear families that would divide the residential space.

Although sometimes living within the same dwelling complex, each smaller unit would cook at its own stove, while acknowledging the common ownership and responsibility for the central ritual room as undivided space.

Orthodox patterns express not only the functional but also the symbolic qualities of a Chinese homestead. Built with an eye to the future, the dwelling suggests more than lifetime occupancy and binds a family to a locale. Family conflict or changes in family fortune frequently would lead to the restructuring of residential space. The fact that so many rural dwellings remain a single rectangle—without a perpendicular wing or two—suggests the frequent frustration of peasant desires for wealth and the fulfilment of the ideal of five generations under one roof.

Fengshui *as Mystical Ecology*

For a millenium, the Chinese have drawn upon the popular yet esoteric set of practices known as *fengshui* to integrate man, his activities, and nature. Sometimes called geomancy and literally meaning 'wind and water', *fengshui* is the notion that alterations of the landscape by man do not simply disturb empty space: they redound to influence, even control, the fortunes of those who intrude. Construction involves risks that demand precautions in order to harness positive forces to one's advantage and also to deflect malevolence. Any change enacts a sequence of reverberations which collectively must be damped in order to reproduce a necessary balance.

The essence of *fengshui* is a universe animated by the interaction of *yin* and *yang* in which an ethereal property known as *qi* ('life breath' or 'cosmic energy') gives character and meaning to a place. Places may be spoken of at an elementary level as exemplifying either *yin* or *yang* characteristics, although sites often exhibit both traits simultaneously. *Yin* places express the female aspect, representing passivity and darkness, and frequently fall away from the sun to the north or north-west. They are optimal for burial. The male or *yang* characteristic expresses brightness and activity by serving the living as suitable sites for individual dwellings or even cities, facing generally southerly or south-easterly. Confusing these natural qualities, many believe, leads to adversity.

A geomancer, armed with instruments and manuals to monitor building sites, provides access to this arcane mystical ecology. The geomancer's principal instrument is a saucer-like block of wood which has at its centre a south-pointing compass surrounded by more than a dozen concentric rings, each of which symbolically represents the ordering of Chinese metaphysics. These include, inter alia, the Eight Trigrams or *bagua*, the duodenary and sexagenary cycles, the location of the nine stars, the twenty-eight constellations, and the five agents. Manipulating these complex rings, the geomancer is able to apply cosmology to matters as practical as house and grave siting.

The *fengshui* characteristics of a site are linked to those people who will utilize it, by relating the time and date of the principal's birth to the particulars of the site. This personalization of time and space enables an individual and his family to draw on the fund of good fortune associated with the site. In a world of limited resources, *fengshui*, many believe, provides a vehicle for ensuring a reasonable share of good fortune that includes wealth, progeny, good harvests, and official positions.

Using visible landscape features and the compass, the geomancer is able to define an auspicious site as one which modulates the flow of *qi*, the ethereal life breath of cosmic energy, thus balancing 'wind' and 'water'. The undulations of intersecting ranges shelter the site and symbolize the comingling of the azure dragon on the east (*yang*) and the white tiger on the west (*yin*), directions which animate *fengshui*. To the east are the azure dragon symbolizing spring, the element wood, and the rising sun. To the south are the vermilion phoenix and the element fire indicating summer. To the west are the white tiger and the element metal symbolizing autumn and harvest. Completing the cycle in the north are the black tortoise and the element water indicating winter. Man is anchored in the soil or earth, the fifth element at the centre of a cosmic map.

Building sites are further selected after the geomancer has considered the shapes of local landscape features representing the five elements of wood, fire, metal, water, and earth. A *fengshui* manual dictates:

on a rock hill you must take an earthy site; on an earth hill you must take a rocky site. Where it is confined, take an open place; where it is open, take a confined space. On a prominence, take the flat; where it is flat, take the prominent. Where strong comes, take weak; where weak comes, take strong. Where there are many hills, emphasize water; where there is much water, emphasize hills ...

Fengshui manuals include abundant diagrams portraying a multiplicity of terrain patterns that might be encountered. Basic hill and water shapes combine in patterned assemblages to define an auspicious site. To heighten the appearance of life-giving *yang*, especially early sunrise and late sunset, care is usually taken so that no part of a dwelling is shaded by hills on the east, south, or west. Hills at the rear are thought necessary not only because they do not block the sun but also because they guard the rear flank. As succinctly stated in the *fengshui* treatise *Yang zhai shishu*, 'to have the front high and the rear low is to be cut off with no family. With the rear high and the front low is to have oxen and horses'. With the building site selected, concern turns to the immediate environs of the prospective house for features that might impact on the lives of those dwelling within. The presence of a water course, pools, rocks, and trees, must be monitored carefully since they presage good or bad fortune.

Much of canonical *fengshui* is comprehensible only to a cosmologically sophisticated geomancer who with 'grand airs and literary pretensions', as the late anthropologist Maurice Freedman tells us, 'puts his metaphysic to common use'. It is clear that those able to avail themselves of the geomancer's diagnostic expertise possess at least a modicum of wealth in order to afford its application. Yet, peasants too have been concerned with worldly benefits as well as the avoidance of misfortune, and thus have been willing to give of their meagre resources to tap the benefits of *fengshui*.

Observations of common houses throughout urban and rural China confirm a widespread understanding of the attributes of *fengshui*. The great range of topographic conditions throughout the country naturally militate against a single pattern of siting because the hilly areas of the south and the open plains of central and northern China present quite different environmental circumstances in which *fengshui* can operate. Yet there is no doubt that even uninitiated farmers site dwellings in

太保相宅圖

Fig. 3.1 An optimal building site, according to basic geomantic concepts, has hills to the rear and a stream to the front, as depicted in this Qing dynasty wood-block print of a geomancer and his assistants choosing a building site. Houses sited in this way 'sit north and face south' (*zuo bei chao nan*) thus protected in winter from cold winds, but open to the sun's passage.

58

broad conformity with *fengshui* criteria using them as rules of thumb rather than restrictive prescriptions.

Practical and recurrent considerations underlie the ritualized behaviour of *fengshui*. A south-facing slope that is protected on the northern side by a set of interlocking mountain ranges provides a building site open to the sun throughout the year and protected in winter from the cold winds characteristic of eastern Asia's climate. *Zuo bei chao nan*, 'sitting north and facing south', has come to be obligatory for Chinese dwellings, temples, and palaces, providing a device for obtaining the best advantage of the regular path of the sun across the sky. The axial arrangement of a house with the ridgepole running east to west controls the degree to which the heat of the sun is seasonally captured or evaded by the south-facing front. These natural conditions may then be fine-tuned by the addition of overhanging eaves, to block the high sun's rays in summer yet permit those low rays of winter to enter.

Building with nature, the practically minded farmer avoids marshy areas and builds where drainage carries water away from the dwelling. Water, like mountain ranges, is seen as a vital element of a site. Chinese farmers have always sought well-drained sites across which water courses to meet their needs for irrigation, cooking, and washing. *Fengshui* manuals prescribe the location of a dwelling near a slow-moving meandering stream so that good influences will be brought to the dwelling. Peasants typically have avoided cutting into a hill because of damage to the pulse of the dragon. These principles help manage and co-ordinate the use of the environment by underscoring elements of the natural order which have worked for generations of forebears.

Mountains are a metaphor for nature and therefore

Fig. 3.2 The immediate environs of a dwelling also demand concern since, many have believed, the lives of the residents would be influenced by features which presage good or bad fortune. This proscription indicates: 'If there is a jade belt stream in front of the gate, this will give rise to high office. Begetting generation after generation of scholars will bring wealth and honour to glorify the house.'

receive prominent attention in *fengshui* manuals. Because not all building sites are bounded by serpentine relief patterns, *fengshui* interpreters and peasants have often been forced to reach to the distant horizon in order to define appropriate contours. Trees and even bamboos are used as a substitute for the rear encircling mountains. Whereas in the West deciduous trees are planted in the front of dwellings for summer shade, in rural China the norm is to place trees behind, where they function more as a windbreak. Until modern times, Chinese houses have generally had windows only on the south facing wall, leaving the rear and sides of the buildings closed to outside influences. The narrow sides of house throughout China that face east and west are called *shanqiang* (mountain walls) which may suggest an attempt to model them after mountains.

Almanacs and Charms

Even the starting date of construction, many have believed, must not be in conflict with the cyclical nomenclature of the household head's birthdate. Annual almanacs (*tongshu* or *quanshu*, 'The book of myriad things') have been produced to help guide peasants through this calendrical labyrinth and provide them with guidance in their dealings with geomancers and craftsmen. Local almanacs are still produced, which use the imperial almanac as a core, and address the needs of ordinary people. Containing not only important astronomical information for ritual purposes, these popular almanacs confirm the agricultural cycle and give auspicious and inauspicious days for countless daily activities. For building purposes such almanacs indicate the dates which should be chosen or avoided and even the lucky and unlucky times for, among other things, breaking ground, raising the pillars, raising the ridgepole, installing a door, and building a kitchen stove—each perceived as critical points demanding of care.

The precautionary attention paid to ground breaking recognizes the fact that forces are alive in the soil that can be harnessed to benefit a household which, if overlooked, will bring disaster. Fruit, incense, packets of vermilion and silver spirit money, accompanied by firecrackers, and candles, have traditionally been offered up to the local tutelary diety, Tudi gong ('the Earth God'), in appeasement for the intended disturbing of the soil, a time when malevolent forces are set free. Chicken blood, believed to be a demon expeller, is often then sprinkled on the building site to restrain such forces. Charms written on slips of peach wood comprise not only readable characters but also arcane calligraphy believed to possess great power. These are addressed to the four cardinal directions (often the centre is included as the fifth direction) as the ground is broken.

Fig. 3.3   Offerings to the four directions, written on slips of peach wood, accompanied by firecrackers and sprinkled chicken blood, prepare the way for ground breaking.

Special attention has always been given to the raising of the wooden frame and the setting into place of the ridge-pole, the most costly components of a house and the critical support for the roof. In eastern Zhejiang province, the raising of the ridgepole traditionally coincided with the occurrence of a high tide or full moon, expressing the hope that the household would be similarly full in prosperity and complete in harmony. It was considered especially fortuitous to raise a ridgepole when there was a light rain since this was a portent for a showering of future riches. Traditionally, a battery of offerings, charms, and talismen were employed in addition, to summon good fortune and to prevent adversity. These practices, which have varied from area to area in China, are not as widespread today as they once were but they can still be observed.

Slips of red paper usually in odd multiples bearing the character *fu* (福) for happiness or good fortune, as well as expressive phrases that evoke auspicious circumstances, may be added to the ridgepole. An early-twentieth-century writer relates how, at least in one area of China, the carpenters 'strike the beam several times with a hammer painted red. This hammer is afterwards presented by the master of the house to a man who has no son; and who if the wished-for-heir is later on born to him, is expected to reward the donor of the hammer by inviting him and his family to a feast'. In this way, the favourable circumstances of housebuilding rebound even to those who assist.

A mirror fixture hung from the beam is an anti-spectral device to protect the inhabitants from demons and ward off all evil influences, while a hanging bamboo sieve is a prophetic indication that many children will be born to the household. Grains of rice may be strewn about or hung in small sacks from the ridgepole to evoke further fertility and prosperity. Sometimes items such as men's trousers and lanterns, which are homophonous with Chinese words for riches or sons, may be suspended as well. In the writing of Chinese characters at this time, care has always been taken to avoid words which include the four dot radical indicating fire, as a precaution against conflagration. Where this is not possible, such words are written incorrectly with only three dots, which signifies water. It is customary for friends and relatives to help celebrate the auspicious occasion of the raising of the ridgepole by bringing gifts of steamed buns, pork, and live chickens. To symbolize abundance, only half of these gifts are eaten that day by those attending while the remaining half are returned.

Although the kitchen stove in a Chinese dwelling has neither the centrality nor the significance of the hearth in the West, care attends its positioning and construction. Once the stove's location is determined, an almanac is consulted to identify an appropriate lucky date on which to install it. In the Hangzhou area of Zhejiang, a cake made of rice and tea leaves together with several coins were traditionally put into the new stove to invoke peace and felicity for the household.

Above the stove in many Chinese homes even today, a

Fig. 3.4 Zaojun, the Kitchen God, has presided over the domestic hearth of most Chinese rural homes, serving as guarantor of household harmony.

niche is constructed for Zaojun, the Kitchen God who presides over the domestic hearth and serves as a guarantor of household harmony and a symbol of domestic unity. Incense is lit daily before his image. Just prior to Chinese New Year, the paper image of Zaojun is burned, sending the god to the Emperor of Heaven to report on the family's behaviour over the past year. With a sugar paste spread on his lips, he is expected to tell only good tales, returning to the house on New Year's Eve. At this time a new picture of him is pasted up on the niche to begin another annual tour of surveillance and protection.

The 'Building Magic' of Craftsmen

Carpenters and masons were traditionally believed capable of carrying out 'building magic' to curse a dwelling and those who occupied it, if they perceived themselves insulted by low pay, poor food, or disrespect. Utilizing information transmitted to them through mnemonic rhymes in the oral tradition as well as information from illustrated manuals, craftsmen might heighten the prospects for good fortune or increase the possibility of evil. Purportedly deriving from Lu Ban, the patron of carpenters and bricklayers, these ideas establish conventions that were recorded in the fifteenth-century *Lu Ban jing* ('Lu Ban manual') and have governed building practices and dimensions down to the present.

To make measurements, carpenters use special rules, calibrated into favourable and unfavourable segments: luck, harm, plunder, office, justice, separation, illness, and wealth. Luck and wealth, found in the end segments, are favourable, office and justice at the centre are acceptable, while the remaining are to be avoided. Used to determine the size of rooms, windows, and doors, these rules have had the effect of standardizing measurements by virtue of avoiding those sections which presage misfortune.

Carpenters might use wooden figures or drawings on paper to effect a curse, with a nail indicating an affliction which would befall the household or its head:

If it pierced the eyes, he would go blind; if it pierced the ears, he would become deaf; if it went through the mouth, he would become dumb; and if it penetrated the heart, then he would die from heart failure. If the figure were hammered onto the door, the master would often be absent and domestic harmony would be destroyed.

Fig. 3.5 Carpenters and masons have traditionally used charms to curse or bless a household. This excerpt from the *Lu Ban jing* ('Lu Ban manual') shows how: *top*, placing a cassia leaf in the column bracket will ensure that descendants of the household head will achieve scholarly success (and thus wealth); *middle*, hiding a boat in the column brackets will guarantee prosperity for the household if the bow is pointed in, but poverty if it is pointed out; *bottom*, long life is ensured for the household if a sprig of pine is secreted anywhere in the house.

Utilizing drawings, dice, knives, and objects made of wood or straw as magic devices, craftsmen could also invoke curses leading to a lack of male descendants, unnatural death, and noise at night, among many others. They were also skilled in methods to bring advantage to a household, if the household's treatment of them was exceptional.

Bricklayers use similar hexes although theirs usually have been made of clay. A pair of clay figures suspended in the chimney by hairs from a horse's tail are believed by some to cause quarrels between husband and wife as the hot air rising from the fire causes the figures to swing and clash against each other. A clay knife pointed at the bedroom or the ancestral hall would lead to murders in the family. Wariness of the tricks of masons and carpenters fostered the need for prescriptive prudence. As a result, the house owner might invoke all-purpose charms as countermeasures to combat whatever curses the craftsmen might have cast.

Summoning Good Fortune

The precautionary 'dos' and 'don'ts' attending the construction of a dwelling are clearly directed at ensuring a household an ample supply of worldly benefits and warranting its domain against misfortune. Much of the folk tradition employed in these exercises is ephemeral, occurring only once, and employing either verbal or written charms that last a relatively short time. Once the dwelling is occupied, the Chinese believe that changing circumstances necessitate continuing attention to the fund that is available for them to tap to ensure good fortune and ward off evil, two central components of happiness. Happiness is a constellation of elements which all orbit around the single Chinese word *fu* (福). Sometimes translated as 'happiness' but better rendered as 'good fortune', 'blessing', or 'luck', *fu* is the intangible power which brings advantage to mankind.

Fig. 3.6 The Chinese character *fu* ('good fortune, happiness, or blessings') appears in many formats as an auspicious declaration as well as an invocation. Here it is emblazoned on a spirit wall.

Around and about dwellings, *fu* is depicted in myriad forms that include not only the ideograph itself but also pictographic representations which are homonyms of *fu*. The bat, an animal generally avoided in the Western world, is welcomed in China as a graceful creature, largely because the word for bat is a homonym of *fu* and thus is emblematic of all that *fu* means. The bat is frequently depicted in such an ornate fashion that it has a striking resemblance to the more graceful butterfly. This confusion plus the fact that a portion of the word for butterfly itself is a near homonym for *fu* has led to the use of the butterfly too as a conventional image for 'good fortune'. Repeated five times in different calligraphic styles, *fu* recalls the five specific components of happiness that may be bestowed: longevity (*shou*), wealth (*fu*), health (*kanging*), love of virtue (*youhaode*), and to die a natural death in old age (*kaozhongming*).

Associated with *fu* is the colour vermilion, auspiciously suggesting summer, the time of life-giving and joy. At the New Year, the character *fu* is emblazoned in black or gold ink on red paper and pasted on the outside of many Chinese gates. Sometimes, this sheet is hung upside down, eliciting from passers-by the comment 'fu is inverted', a homophone for 'fu has arrived'. A horizontal strip of red paper with the characters *wu fu lin men* (五福臨門 'the five good fortunes have arrived at the door') is frequently hung above the lintel as an invocation for the arrival of happiness. To accompany such a horizontal strip are vertically hung parallel couplets which express similar sentiments of hope drawn with poetic imagery. Attached in pairs to the front gate and placed also in the main room of the house throughout China, couplets express an extraordinary range of subject matter.

The Chinese honour age and desire a long life in order to enjoy the bestowal of blessings as one ages. It is not suprising then that the character *shou* (壽 'longevity'), as well as symbols to represent it, are common ornamental motifs about dwellings. The character *wan* (萬 '10,000'), ornamentally drawn as a backwards swastika, expresses the same notion of eternal life. Chinese legends abound with the quests of Daoist priests for recipes to ensure immortality. Short of eternal life, however, Chinese traditionally have desired to live at least to the age of sixty, completing five cycles of the twelve-year zodiac. Common symbols and representations of longevity are the crane, evergreen trees, rocks, the peach, tortoise, and deer.

Fig. 3.7 Symbols to represent the wish for a long life as well as the Chinese character *shou* ('longevity') itself are common decorative motifs in Chinese dwellings. Here, carved into a lattice panel are two cranes, an evergreen tree, and rocks—all symbols of long life.

Within the 'five good fortunes', aside from longevity only wealth is directly or indirectly depicted in common folk ornamental motifs. Neither health, love of virtue, nor dying a natural death in old age find emblematic representation, perhaps because of the fact that they are relatively abstract and not easily depicted symbolically. On the other hand, wealth (*fu* 富) is not only real, it is an obvious homonym for generic good fortune (*fu* 福), that composite notion which includes wealth as but only one of its five components. It is not surprising then that it is the attainment of riches that is evoked in many Chinese minds when the homophone *fu* is uttered. The written forms also share a similarity that is frequently confused in the mind of the unlettered.

Although wealth could be acquired through commerce or ownership of land, traditionally the socially accepted source of wealth was official position, a status normally acquired by long years of study, the passing of exacting examinations, and the attainment of degrees. *Lu* (祿) is the Chinese word used to link official position with the emoluments which flow from such a status. Wealth obviously can be represented directly as forms of money, whether round coins with a square hole in the centre, cowrie shells, axes, spades, knives, or concave ingots that have served as currency at one time or another in Chinese history.

The difficult quest necessary for passing examinations and achieving financial advantage is epitomized by the carp, a fish that must struggle against the currents, to reach Longmen, the Dragon Gate. The carp is said to metamorphose into a mighty dragon just as a common person can be transformed via the examination route into a successful scholar-official. The depiction of any fish, indeed, is a claim to prosperity understood by all Chinese, because of the homonymic relationship between the characters *yu* representing both fish and abundance.

The triad of *fu*, *shou*, and *lu* ('good fortune, longevity, and emolument') was anthropomorphized over a long period of time into three individuals whose symbolic images ornament the interior of many dwellings. These characters evolved as emblems in the élite culture, but by the Ming dynasty, each had secured a footing in folk imagery as well. Their enduring popularity reflects their non-sectarian status outside the pantheons of Buddhism, Confucianism, or Daoism. The Chinese popularly refer to them as 'stellar gods' (*xing*). Each has a peculiar characterization which makes them immediately recognizable whether depicted in a simple paper cut-out affixed to a wall, in a colourful woodblock print, or in a more elaborate three-dimensional carving made of wood or clay.

Harmony at home and a wish for numerous descendants round out the common themes which are represented ornamentally about a dwelling. Marital bliss is depicted from the animal realm as a pair of fish swimming in stylized water, as magpies entwined on a branch, or as a pair of flying geese. In the plant world the narcissus, orchid, and the lotus carry the same meaning of conjugal happiness. Marital concord and sexual union are represented by the depiction of the lotus stem and the lotus pod. A similar theme is respresented by the celestial twins He He, one carrying a lotus and the other a box, all elements which share the homonym *he* for harmony.

Offspring in great numbers are considered to be the purpose of marriage and are the subject of substantial folk ornamentation. The joy associated with birth was traditionally reserved for the arrival of a son, considered a *da xi* or 'major happiness' while the birth of a daughter was a *xiao xi* or 'small happiness'. Folk symbols referring to children do not always specify gender, but implicitly sons are what is desired. *Zi* is the Chinese phoneme for seed, child, and son. Thus pomegranates, watermelons, bottle-gourds or calabash, and lotus pods which contain abundant seeds, serve to evoke the notion of fertility and male progeny.

Protection against Misfortune

It has not always been enough simply to summon good fortune, emoluments, and longevity, the manifold conditions of a good life. Traditionally the use of precautionary charms to protect the household has been thought necessary to dispel evil. These preliminary efforts are employed at the time a dwelling is constructed while others are added and renewed as circumstances dictate.

Mirrors and the Eight Trigrams or *bagua* symbol are sometimes added as antidotes for possible evil influences that may arise from location or subsequent building nearby. The Eight Trigrams, comprising the sets of three lines of the celebrated *Yijing*, can reflect the adverse effects of bad planning. These are especially used in situations considered 'mutually antagonistic' such as where one door would face another across a lane, or a lane leads

Fig. 3.8 As anti-spectral devices, a mirror and three tridents are sometimes placed above the door.

Fig. 3.9 The face of a tiger, an eight trigrams diagram, and an incantation invoking the protection of Mount Tai are placed on the facades of dwellings throughout China as an amulet to guard the dwelling and family from misfortune.

directly to a doorway. A small mirror, radiating *yang*, is usually hung above the door where it is seen by many Chinese as a potent deflector of malevolent influences.

The face of a tiger, the third animal of the Chinese zodiac and a *yang* creature, is sometimes hung as an amulet to guard the resources of a household by driving off demons and malignant spirits. The face is frequently combined with other symbols to multiply the protective effect.

Protection may be enhanced by affixing a pair of door gods to the doors. Facing each other and in full battle garb, these fierce warriors are there to ensure the safety and inviolability of the dwelling. Especially common with urban houses but found with village dwellings as well are *yingbi*, also called *zhaobi*, or spirit walls of brick or wood. Placed just inside the gate the *yingbi* are believed by some Chinese to be capable of deflecting negative elements that travel only in straight lines.

On the fifth day of the fifth lunar month, *yin* or negative elements are believed to emerge. These include those 'ghosts' responsible for disease, accidental death, and financial disaster. The so-called five noxious or poisonous creatures—the snake, the centipede, the scorpion, the gecko, and the toad or spider—are said to proliferate at this time. On this day people throughout China still take precautions against these ghosts that include the hanging of pungent plant stalks that are said to repel evil, the pasting up on their door of a print of the demon queller Zhong Kui, or fanciful calligraphy which casts a kind of spell.

A stone pillar inscribed with the characters *shi gandang* (石敢當 'stone dares to resist evil') or *Taishan shi gandang* (泰山石敢當 'stone of Mount Tai dares to resist evil'), and *Jiang Taigong zai ci* (姜太公在此 'Jiang Taigong is here') might be placed near the house to serve as an external line of defence. Taishan, the most eminent of China's mountains, located in Shandong province, contains stone believed to have great power. Although slabs of such stone or even local stone are believed to be potent, the words themselves are today accepted as sufficient. Taken collectively, these charms portray a desire to make inviolate the inner space of family life by keeping at bay those malevolent elements belonging to a different spatial domain.

Throughout Chinese history, sites have been selected and dwellings built based upon images of an organic view of the cosmos that includes even the mundane tasks associated with providing a habitat. These efforts typify the Chinese folk tradition and demonstrate those factors which tie the individual, family, and society and link them symbolically to the past. Recognizing and employing auspicious numbers and directions, 'wind and water interpreters' and craftsmen have been able to warrant to those living in a household, long-term benefits accruing from location and ritual. These practices remain visibly popular in Taiwan, Singapore, and Hong Kong. They survive as well throughout the mainland, where official policy rails out against superstitious practices while the peasantry in the countryside continue to acknowledge a tradition of great relevance. Applied ornamentation as well as that carved in wood, stone, and brick throughout Chinese dwellings reveals a tenacious concern for material happiness for the family.

4

Trends in Contemporary China

AFTER many years—perhaps even a century or more—of neglect and decay, a veritable house building boom has been under-way in China over the past decade on account of unparalleled rural prosperity. Indeed, the records show that more housing was built in China between 1979 and 1985 than in the previous thirty years; this pace continues to the present. Chinese rural households have moved quickly to make up for decades of deprivation, satisfying pent-up demand with a flush of consumerism that includes house building. In the decades after 1949, much urban and rural housing became increasingly dilapidated because of poor maintenance and vandalism, as well as the pressure of providing shelter for increasing numbers of people. This recent transformation has brought with it not only the replacement of old structures with new ones in the name of progress but also, less radically, the 'modernization' of old dwellings.

In spite of the fact that much new housing construction is 'Chinese modern', that is hybrid in style, building techniques, and materials used, dwellings generally continue to be fashioned after traditional designs, utilizing building materials and practices common in China for millennia. In some cases, such as with active solar houses, truly revolutionary designs have found their way into the countryside. A good deal of this new building however is technically flawed and deficient, lacking the aesthetic appeal of the finer dwellings built earlier. New home owners commonly complain of poor workmanship and materials. Architects are designing some improved dwellings, the plans of which are finding their way into the countryside via copy books. Provincial and national housing design competitions have challenged many to confront tradition and introduce innovative ways to improve Chinese living space.

The strength of precedent continues to play a compelling role in the design and construction of rural housing. Yet increasing income levels and technology are affecting the structural components and building techniques used throughout China as is the popularization of new designs. Because villagers generally build the best house they can afford, it is not surprising that as per capita incomes have risen, the use of more durable and costly building materials has increased as well. Although there is probably more housing of better quality and with improved amenities today than has ever existed in China, it is equally true that rarely does a new house match the elegance of

Fig. 4.1 In a national competition in 1981, a first prize was given to this design for a duplex in south China. The design is remarkably similar to the Han dynasty funerary model shown in Fig. 1.2.

materials or scale characteristic of the best of dwellings built in the past.

Masons and carpenters, like owners and contractors themselves, are searching for materials and methods which are new and modern as well as reasonably priced and efficient that do not clash with inherited patterns. It is an indisputable fact, however, that the long slack period in residential construction in China has meant that the skill of craftsmen has deteriorated substantially, and modern solutions to old problems are being pursued without the experience and technical or design ability to address them adequately. In an effort to pick up the slack, countless unskilled workers, in search of high pay and a trade, are learning on the job or in fewer cases as apprentices to once-skilled building craftsmen.

Shortages of timber, the high cost of wood, and government policies which encourage the substitution of other materials for wood, have led to a dramatic decrease in the use of wood in housing, not only for structural members but also for decoration. Instead the thin inexpensive bricks utilized in the past, masons today lay larger fired bricks in traditional box bonds. Pillars made of concrete reinforced with steel rods are increasingly being used instead of wooden pillars if the owners intend that the building will eventually reach three or four floors. Fired bricks can then be added either as a freestanding curtain wall between the load-bearing concrete pillars or to support the roof and upper floors directly.

Other components made of cement, including lintels, purlins, and stairs, as well as window and door frames, have multiplied also, accepted readily because of their durability and relatively low cost. Formed concrete foundations are slowly taking the place of widely available stone. Perhaps the most ubiquitous prefabricated building components made of cement are slabs of pre-stressed concrete that are used to span the open space between the walls. Varying in dimensions depending on the width of the *jian*, such slabs provide a floor panel for each upper storey that does not require supporting joists. Usually made locally, their overall weight is lightened by the multiple hollow cores which characterize them. Used together with reinforced concrete pillars, they make the construction of multiple storey dwellings possible.

There is a continuing widespread use of traditional brick-and tile-making technologies. These simple processes are still widely used not only because they draw upon abundantly available labour and soil resources but because they produce a reasonable product at relatively low cost. Furthermore, the production of clay bricks and tiles can be controlled locally without the interference of higher level authorities who regulate the availability of cement, wood, and steel rods, building materials that are often in short supply in most areas of the country.

The sheer volume of brick and tile production in recent years, however, has meant that valuable arable land often has to be used to supply the necessary raw materials. The deleterious impact of these developments on farmland, itself in short supply in China, has often been described in the press. Signs erected in the countryside warn about the dangers of removing valuable soil from cropland to make brick and tile. This attention has led some even to claim that 'land saving is as important as family planning'. This has spurred a proliferation of multi-storey dwellings throughout the country 'borrowing the sky instead of the land' as some Chinese describe it.

Important changes taking place in the Chinese family are having an impact on housing, a result of both new socio-economic conditions and government policies. In

China today, there is a clear tendency for each newly married couple to establish its own independent household rather than share living space with that of the husband's family as has been traditional Chinese practice. Furthermore, reflecting the government's population policy encouraging the one-child family, there has been an overall trend towards smaller families. This movement toward nuclear families has brought with it a parallel change in the nature of houses.

No longer is the idealized norm a ramified structure, the proverbial manse with many interconnected rooms capable of housing as many as 'five generations under one roof'. Today it is the single family dwelling that has captured the imagination of Chinese home-makers and home builders. Throughout China one sees parents continuing to live in their old dwelling while building and outfitting a new house for their adult children. A concession perhaps for separation, is proximity, since parents and married children often live in adjacent dwellings or nearby.

Today there are constraints on the amount of land-space a house can occupy. Building-space for new houses is allocated by village and township governments on the basis of household size, except in the case of building lots occupied by existing houses and where planning is weak. Nevertheless, a preoccupation with bigness, the building of a dwelling whose capacity goes beyond that of residence, is still apparent in the countryside. The use of glazed tiles, larger windows, and lights now brightens many kitchens, making it possible for this heavily used room to be better ventilated and cleaner than ever before. Improved toilets and bathrooms however are slow in being introduced into even the more expensive rural homes.

Fig. 4.2 Two-storey dwellings with common orientation in compact settlements, are proliferating throughout rural China, even in north China where they were not found in the past. Often using substantial cement and other new building technologies, they are generally airier, more spacious, and brighter than traditional dwellings. Huairuo county, Beijing.

Numerous provincial and several national rural housing design competitions have been held since 1979 to encourage improvements in rural habitats by drawing upon the expertise of architects, builders, and homeowners. Increasingly, efforts have been made to incorporate local architectural traditions, improved materials, and a better use of space in the designs. Efforts are also being directed at improving lighting, ventilation, and sanitation within dwellings as well as providing space for supplementary production activities.

Glossary

Bagua. The Eight Trigrams.

Chuandou. Pillars–and–transverse tie beams; wooden structural framework.

Da xi. 'A major happiness'; birth of a son.

Fengshui. Geomancy or mystical ecology; literally 'wind and water'.

Fu. Good fortune; blessings; happiness.

Fu. Wealth.

Hangtu. Tamped earth, used for wall construction.

He. Harmony.

Hipped roof. A roof with sloping sides and ends.

Jian. A bay or construction module; the space between columns.

Kangning. Health.

Jiang Taigong zai ci. 'Jiang Taigong is here'.

Kang. An elevated platform made of earthen bricks which serves as a bed in north China. Heat passes from the cooking stove through flues to heat it.

Kao zhong ming. To die a natural death.

Liangzhu. Pillars–and–beams wooden structural framework.

Lintel. The horizontal crosspiece over a window or door whose purpose is to carry the weight of the wall above.

Lu. Official emolument; wealth.

Matou qiang. 'Horse's head walls'; stepped gable walls.

Purlin. A piece of timber laid horizontally to support the rafters of a roof.

Qi. An ethereal quality; 'life breath' or 'cosmic energy' that is the focus of *fengshui*.

Ridgepole. Horizontal beam running the length of the highest point of a double sloping roof.

Shanqiang. 'Mountain walls'; the gable ends of a Chinese building.

Shou. Longevity.

Siheyuan. The classical northern courtyard house.

Tailiang. Pillars–and–beams wooden structural framework.

Taishan shi gandang. 'The stone of Mount Tai dares to resist evil'.

Tongshu. Annual almanac; 'The Book of Myriad Things'; also *quanshu.*

Truss. Triangular framework or structure to support a roof.

Wan. Ten thousand; longevity.

Wu fu lin men. 'The Five Good Fortunes have arrived at the door'.

Xiao xi. 'A minor happiness' birth of a daughter.

Xing. Stellar god.

Xuanshan ding. 'Overhanging gables' style roof profile.

Yin and *yang.* Complementary opposites.

Yingbi. Spirit wall.

Yingshan ding. 'Firm mountain' roof profile with no roof overhang in the gable area.

Youhaode. Love of virtue.

Zhaobi. Spirit wall.

Zi. Chinese phoneme for seed, child, and son.

Zuo bei chao nan. 'Sitting north and facing south'; the near obligatory orientation for a Chinese building.

Select Bibliography

Blaser, Werner, *Courtyard Houses in China: Tradition and Present*, Basel, Birkhauser Verlag, 1979.

Dillingham, Reed, and Chang-lin Dillingham, *Survey of Traditional Architecture of Taiwan*, Taizhong, Tunghai University, 1971.

Clément, Sophie, Pierre Clément, and Shin Yang-hak, *Architecture du Paysage en Extrême Orient*, Paris, Ecole Nationale Superieure des Beaux-Arts and Editions Berger-Levrault, 1987.

Feuchtwang, Stephen, *An Anthropological Analysis of Chinese Geomancy*, Vientiane, Vithangna, 1974.

Freedman, Maurice, 'Geomancy', *Proceedings, Royal Anthropological Institute of Great Britain and Ireland, 1968*, London, Royal Anthropological Society, 1969.

Fuller, Myron L. and Frederick G. Clapp, 'Loess and Rock Dwellings in Shensi, China', *Geographical Review*, Vol. 14, 1924.

Hommel, Rudolf P., *China at Work*, New York, John Day, 1937.

Knapp, Ronald G., *China's Traditional Rural Architecture: A Cultural Geography of the Common House*, Honolulu, University of Hawaii Press, 1986.

—— *China's Vernacular Architecture: House Form and Culture*, Honolulu, University of Hawaii Press, 1989.

—— 'Chinese Rural Dwellings in Taiwan', *Journal of Cultural Geography*, Vol. 3, 1982.

—— 'Taiwan's Vernacular Architecture', *Orientations*, Vol. 12, 1981.

Lee, Chien-lang, *Jinmen minju jianzhu* (A survey of Jinmen (Kinmen) domestic architecture), Taibei, Beiwu chubanshe, 1978.

—— *Taiwan jianzhu shi* (History of the architecture of Taiwan), Taibei, Beiwu chubanshe, 1980.

Lin, Heng-tao, 'Taiwan's Traditional Chinese Houses', *Echo*, Vol. 5, 1975.

Liu, Dunzhen, *Zhongguo zhuzhai gaishuo* (Introduction to Chinese dwellings), Beijing, Jianzhu gongcheng chubanshe, 1957. (Translated into French as *La Maison Chinoise*, Paris, Bibliotheque Berger-Levrault, 1980).

Palmer, Martin, ed., *T'ung Shu: The Ancient Chinese Almanac*, Boston, Shambhala, 1986.

Ruitenbeek, Klaas, 'Craft and Ritual in Traditional Chinese Carpentry', *Chinese Science*, Vol. 7, 1986.

—— *The Lu Ban jing: A Fifteenth Century Chinese Carpenter's Manual*, Leiden, Brill (forthcoming).

Spencer, Joseph E., 'The Houses of the Chinese', *Geographical Review*, Vol. 37, 1947.

Sullivan, Linda F., 'Traditional Chinese Regional Architecture: Chinese Houses', *Journal of the Royal Asiatic Society of Great Britain and Ireland, Hong Kong Branch*, Vol. 12, 1972.

von Poseck, Helena, 'How John Chinaman Builds His House', *East of Asia Magazine*, Vol. 4, 1905.

Useful books in Chinese with extensive illustrations have been produced in recent years by China Building Materials Press (Zhonguo jianzhu gongye chubanshe), Beijing, on individual Chinese provinces, including Fujian, Jilin, Yunnan, and Zhejiang. Others are promised in this series.

Index

CHINA

XINJIANG UYGUR
Autonomous Region

QINGHAI

TIBET
Autonomous Region